Toil and Toxics

Toil and Toxics

Workplace Struggles and
Political Strategies for
Occupational Health

James C. Robinson

UNIVERSITY OF CALIFORNIA PRESS
BERKELEY LOS ANGELES LONDON

University of California Press
Berkeley and Los Angeles, California

University of California Press, Ltd.
London, England

© 1991 by
The Regents of the University of California

Library of Congress Cataloging-in-Publication Data

Robinson, James C. (James Claude), 1953–
    Toil and toxics : workplace struggles and political strategies
for occupational health / James C. Robinson.
        p. cm.
    Includes index.
    ISBN 0–520–08448–9
    1. Occupational diseases. 2. Pollution. 3. Environmental
health. 4. Industrial hygiene—Political aspects—United States.
5. Industrial toxicology—Political aspects—United States.
I. Title.
RC967.R63 1991
363.11'0973—dc20   90–20986
                                                             CIP

Printed in the United States of America

9 8 7 6 5 4 3 2 1

Contents

List of Tables

Acknowledgments

Writing a book is in many ways a solitary and private affair. As Simone de Beauvoir might have said, the author must personally confront the fear of the blank computer screen. A book like this one, however, is composed on a public stage, coming out of years of discussion at Berkeley and elsewhere. I am indebted to the institutions and organizations that have facilitated this dialogue and forced me repeatedly to revise my views of how the world works and how it might be made to work better. The Institute of Industrial Relations provided financial support and a home away from home. A Special Emphasis Research Career Award from the National Institute for Occupational Safety and Health made possible the more recent statistical analyses. Most important among the institutions has been the Center for Occupational and Environmental Health, which created my faculty position at the University of California and which continues to provide the colleagues and the context for my work in health policy.

This book has been a collective endeavor. Numerous graduate students and postdoctoral fellows have contributed their ideas, energies, and algorithms, and without them I would never have been able to carry through. In particular I must thank Dalton Paxman, Cathy Weinberger, Ruth Oscar, Kris Calvin, Edward Feasel, Laura Brown, Josh Reilly, Glenn Shor, JoAnna Omi, Mita Giacomini, Susan Gabbard, Keun Lee, and Jason Bai. Many of these individuals have gone on to bigger and better things. Some professors have also gotten in their

xii   *Acknowledgments*

licks; Alan Derickson and Burt Loudan saved me several embarrassments and pointed me in some new directions.

I owe the most to Bill Pease and Juliann Sum. Bill argued me through three complete restructurings of the text and helped me shake off a narrow syndicalist perspective on collective action in favor of one more sympathetic to social regulation. Juliann Sum took on the penultimate draft, when my ego was already bruised and my mood prickly. After she edits a chapter, it is hard to discern whether the text was printed in black ink and marked with red comments or printed in red ink and marked with black comments. If any passage remains vague or any point unsubstantiated, it is due to my obdurate refusal to take all the good advice I was given.

Introduction:
Working and Living
with Poison

It began with a brief announcement in July of 1977. Ten employees of a pesticide mixing plant in California's agricultural heartland had been made sterile by workplace exposure to a pesticide called dibromochloropropane, DBCP for short. The story quickly got into newspaper headlines as more workers were found to be sterile, the chemical was linked to the risk of cancer, it turned up on fruit in grocery stores, and public water supplies throughout the state proved to be contaminated. Labor and environmental groups pushed for a ban on the manufacture and use of the chemical. The labor union representing the sterile workers began to demand from other employers full information on the toxic substances used on the shop floor. This helped ignite a nationwide "right-to-know" movement that soon spread from the workplace to the community at large. The DBCP controversy stands out as a landmark case in society's struggle to come to terms with the health risks of substances that are central to many production processes in the economy.[1]

What so distinguished the DBCP issue, however, was the manner in which the toxic properties of the pesticide came to light. As early as the 1950s scientific studies sponsored by the manufacturers had produced strong evidence of reproductive toxicity in laboratory animals. The studies suggested that protective procedures and monitoring of exposed workers were advisable, but the employers took no such steps. The findings remained confidential until they were published in a scientific journal in 1961, and then were largely ignored until the furor broke out sixteen years later. Several governmental agencies had been studying the possibility that DBCP caused cancer, but had not taken any action. Those who blew the whistle on DBCP were not the managers of the companies producing it, not the corporate scientists, and not the governmental regulatory agencies, but rather the exposed workers themselves.

The DBCP problem came to light as a result of a year-long effort by a group of chemical workers and their labor union. In January 1976 the leadership of the Oil, Chemical, and Atomic Workers International Union (OCAW) distributed a health and safety questionnaire to workers in the Agricultural Chemical Department of the Occidental Chemical plant in Lathrop where DBCP was being produced. In March, the local union sought aid from the national union's health and safety staff, who requested the right to conduct an industrial hygiene survey at Lathrop. Management denied this request. The union analyzed the results of the worker survey and presented to management a series of specific demands for improvements in working conditions, based on the workers' reports. Up to this point, however, there were no complaints of sterility, and the union did not focus on that issue.

The first complaints of difficulty in fathering children came to the attention of the union in July 1976. In August the union decided that the complaints should be evaluated by collecting and analyzing semen samples, and began the slow process of convincing individual workers. Throughout the fall and winter the union also requested from management the identities of the chemical materials being used in the formulation of the pesticide, plus all relevant toxicological and industrial hygiene information. Occidental Chemical divulged nothing at this time. In March 1977 management formally denied the union's request for a workplace industrial hygiene evaluation and for the medical monitoring of individual workers. In the spring of 1977, the union brought the problem to the attention of a group of filmmakers interested in producing a documentary on occupational health and safety issues. Together the lo-

cal union and the filmmakers obtained semen samples and
had them analyzed. When the initial samples revealed sterility, the union requested an investigation by the National Institute for Occupational Safety and Health (NIOSH). It was at
this point that public attention focused on the issue and that
the plant management changed its position to one of full cooperation in testing for health effects.

The response of the regulatory agencies to the events at
Lathrop was rapid but uncoordinated. Various environmental
protection and public health agencies imposed restrictions to
discourage firms from manufacturing DBCP. The California
Department of Food and Agriculture, which was primarily responsive to farmer and chemical industry concerns, sought
ways to allow continued use of the pesticide. The department's approach nearly succeeded but was undermined by
the continuing revelations concerning DBCP. The events at
Lathrop had spurred medical testing programs for workers
exposed to DBCP elsewhere in the nation and, indeed, around
the world. Sterility was reported among chemical workers in
Colorado, Arkansas, Israel, Costa Rica, and Mexico. Residues
of DBCP were found on peaches, grapes, and citrus fruits being sold to consumers, raising the question of whether the
health effects of DBCP might extend beyond industrial and agricultural workers. The final blow, however, came when high
levels of DBCP were measured in public water supplies, first
in Lathrop and then throughout the San Joaquin Valley. These
revelations created an atmosphere of crisis and led to a strong
regulatory response. The Occupational Safety and Health Administration (OSHA) set a permissible exposure limit for the
workplace of one part DBCP per billion parts of air. The Environmental Protection Agency (EPA) banned the application of
the pesticide to almost all crops in the United States.

The DBCP story did not end there, however. While EPA had
banned most applications of the pesticide, nothing prevented
its manufacture, provided OSHA's exposure limits were met.
Furthermore, nothing prevented its application to crops in
other countries. The major U.S. producers of DBCP, including

Dow Chemical, Shell, and Occidental Chemical, did stop production. Production expanded, however, first in Mexico and
then at a small Californian firm named AMVAC. The contrast
between AMVAC and the former producers of DBCP could not
have been more striking. The original producers were large
corporations with considerable assets, sophisticated industrial hygiene departments, and stable, largely unionized work
forces. AMVAC was a small company in perilous financial
straits, with only limited insurance coverage, and with a tran-
sient, nonunion work force. AMVAC soon ran afoul of the regulatory agencies, receiving citations both for chemical spills
inside the plant and for venting the pesticide into the general
atmosphere.

Meanwhile, the Oil, Chemical, and Atomic Workers union
was pursuing its efforts at the Lathrop plant and elsewhere in
the country where it represented chemical workers. Although
the production of DBCP stopped at Lathrop, the production
of many other agricultural chemicals continued. The union
sought and obtained a list of all substances used and produced in the plant, a new ventilation system in the Agricultural Chemical Department, personal protective equipment
for individual workers, periodic medical examinations for all
workers in the plant, and the maintenance of pay and seniority levels for workers forced to change jobs for occupational
health reasons. The union also coordinated the filing of Workers' Compensation claims and legal actions on the part of individual sterile workers.

The OCAW initiated a right-to-know campaign at all the
chemical plants where it had members. In some instances
management responded promptly with information on what
was being produced, the levels at which workers were exposed, and possible toxic effects of the chemicals. In other
cases, however, management refused to give this information
to the union, claiming it was confidential. The union pursued
a number of recalcitrant employers before the National Labor
Relations Board (NLRB), successfully claiming that this information was essential if unions were to represent adequately the interests of their members in the collective bar-

gaining process. These cases were of particular importance in facilitating growth in collective bargaining for improvements in health and safety conditions and in instigating community efforts to gain access to chemical hazard data.

The right-to-know movement soon grew beyond the collective bargaining arena. Individual cities, counties, and states began to mandate that firms operating within their jurisdictions reveal the identity of the chemicals being used and their possible health effects. These right-to-know statutes sometimes focused on workplace exposures and industrial workers but often extended to environmental exposures and the entire citizenry. The logic of the movement soon drove it beyond a focus on information to the worker's and citizen's "right to act" to prevent toxic emissions and exposures. Shop floor concerns gradually merged into the political struggle over the government's responsibility for protecting public health and the environment.

A number of themes emerged from the DBCP incident that proved to be important for the larger debate over occupational and environmental health. The Lathrop workers had no access to the available scientific evidence on the toxicity of the chemical they worked with, and therefore continued to be exposed until the adverse health effects became widespread. Once their suspicions were aroused, individual workers were able to turn to their labor union for help in investigating and ameliorating the problem. The DBCP experience and others similar to it generated a nationwide movement to guarantee worker and community access to information on toxic substances. DBCP production soon shifted, however, from the unionized and highly paid work force at Occidental Chemical to the nonunion and low-paid work force at AMVAC. The ultimate reduction in DBCP use occurred primarily because of concerns for environmental degradation and the health of the public, as expressed in the OSHA and EPA regulations.

The themes of the DBCP tragedy are the themes of this book. The unifying focus is on worker choices among alternative strategies for controlling occupational health and safety hazards. These alternatives consist of individual decisions to quit dangerous jobs, collective struggles for improved conditions, legal battles to require disclosure of information and prevent discrimination against health and safety activists, and political campaigns to mobilize the standards-setting and enforcement powers of government. In documenting worker and management initiatives on the shop floor and in the labor market, the book analyzes a wealth of statistical information on workers, firms, labor unions, and working conditions spanning the thirty-year period between the late 1950s and the late 1980s. In documenting the legal and political struggles over the right to know, the right to act, and the direct regulation of toxic substances, the book uses extensive materials on grass-roots movements, state and national legislation, judicial interpretations, and activities of regulatory agencies.

The focus on strategies and choices is particularly important at this time because the United States is engaged in a major debate over the appropriate social response to the risks posed by toxic substances. Throughout much of the twentieth century there existed a social consensus that collective organizations such as labor unions and public institutions such as the courts and regulatory agencies had a legitimate and important role to play in mediating conflicts between employers and employees. This consensus was evident in the public support for private collective bargaining concerning health and safety, as embodied in the rulings of the National Labor Relations Board. It was evident in the court orders that eroded the employer's right to conceal hazard information and to fire employees who disclosed toxic emissions or refused to perform exceptionally hazardous assignments. The consensus was most evident, perhaps, in the bipartisan support for the 1970 legislation that created the Occupational Safety and Health Administration to enforce standards limiting toxic exposures throughout private industry.

This social consensus has completely unraveled. Beginning in the 1970s and accelerating in the 1980s, an alternative perspective has questioned the legitimacy of labor unions, judicial activism, and social regulation. It has revived a libertarian conception of the labor market as the domain of voluntary transactions between equal partners and linked this with an economic view of market competition as providing the strongest incentives for improving working conditions. This ideology is suspicious or hostile toward labor unions, supportive of management's prerogative to hire and fire at will, and vehemently opposed to government regulation. It sees individual quits and job shopping as the only legitimate worker strategy for achieving safer working conditions, and seeks to eliminate the alternatives.

This intellectual backlash against a half century of public support for workers' rights mirrors developments in the economic and political spheres. In the labor market, employers have abandoned their earlier acceptance of collective bargaining and have aggressively undermined labor unions and the possibility for collective workplace strategies. In the courtroom, liberal judges are being replaced by conservatives who adopt a more limited view of workers' rights and the role of the judiciary in upholding them. In Washington, the Occupational Safety and Health Administration was nearly destroyed by a president who viewed social regulation of toxic substances, rather than toxic substances themselves, as the problem to be controlled.

As the 1990s unfold, this ideology of private power and public acquiescence is generating its own backlash. Worker and citizen concern for the health risks and ecological effects of toxic substances is at its peak. Labor unions are coming to view health and safety as a major organizing theme. More important, perhaps, toxics populism is emerging as a potent political movement. Communities throughout the nation have become angry over toxic wastes in the air, in the water, and on the land. Consumer-product labeling and toxic-emissions reporting requirements have built on workplace right-to-know efforts. The courts are filled with plaintiffs demanding reductions of emissions and compensation for damages. The regulatory agencies are under intense pressure to shake off their lethargy and provide leadership for society's efforts to control toxic substances.

Our time is one of difficult choices among alternative strategies. In each case workers and citizens must choose whether to pursue their best options as individuals or form organizations to extend their reach. They must decide whether to focus on private strategies such as job shopping, consumer boycotts, and collective bargaining or on public strategies channeled through the courts and the regulatory agencies. Most important, they must choose whether to pursue a single strategy with all the resources at their disposal or spread their efforts across a mix of strategies that offer different possibilities. In making these choices the best guide is the experience gained through earlier social efforts, from the successes and failures of particular strategies in particular contexts. By providing a historical, economic, and political analysis of worker efforts to control workplace hazards, this book hopes to contribute to the development of more effective public health and environmental strategies in the years to come.

1

Alternative Strategies for Controlling Workplace Hazards

Our understanding of occupational health and safety is bedeviled by conflicting images of workers and the working environment. Some evoke an individualistic image of the worker as rational agent, aggressively pursuing his or her self-interest in the labor market or before a court of law. Others describe the individual worker as unaware and powerless and emphasize the importance of collective efforts mediated by labor unions and governmental regulatory agencies. This contrast between individual and collective action is superimposed upon a contrast between the private and the public. For some, the workplace and the labor market are the domain of free contracting between equals; social ends are best achieved by respecting the working conditions implicitly agreed to by individual workers choosing among job options and explicitly agreed to by labor unions engaged in collective bargaining. For others, the private economy is the source of exploitation and injustice; social ends are best achieved through courts and regulatory agencies established by political processes.

The truth, of course, lies between these extremes. Workers are neither ignorant nor omniscient, neither apathetic nor omnipotent. They do not always show solidarity with their fellows, but neither do they always quit at the first sign of danger. The labor market is not an "Eden of the innate rights of man," but neither is it merely a veil over a shop floor of relentless exploitation and wage slavery. The courts and the regulatory agencies are not undiluted expressions of the popular will, but neither are they merely the instruments of special interest groups. The contrasts between individual and collective action and between the private and public spheres are historically conditioned and change in response to changes in cultural norms and political power. For all their limitations, however, these contrasts can serve a useful conceptual purpose. Together, they create a two-by-two matrix that embodies the range of available strategies for controlling occupational health and safety hazards. The four alternative strategies are presented in graphic form in table 1. Workers can pursue their individual "exit" options in the private economy, quitting hazardous jobs and searching for safe ones. Collectively they can pursue union "voice" strategies and bargain privately with employers for safer conditions. Dissatisfied with the opportunities available in the private marketplace, individual workers can pursue their legal rights before a public court of law. Collectively they can support public statutes

Table 1
*A Framework for Understanding
Worker Strategies to Control Workplace Hazards*

	Individual	*Collective*
Private	The Exit Strategy: Searching for safe working conditions; quitting hazardous jobs	The Voice Strategy: Joining labor unions; bargaining with employers for improved conditions
Public	The Legal Strategy: Suing in court for individual rights to know and rights to act	The Regulatory Strategy: Organizing politically to support governmental regulation of toxic substances

and standards that regulate working conditions across wide sectors of industry.

This chapter uses the four-part matrix as the structure for a theory of how workers respond to health and safety hazards within a given economic and political system and how, in turn, their responses influence the broader system. The conceptual framework is presented here in schematic form and will be expanded throughout the book. The statistical and historical data that support the theory will be treated in following chapters. An overview of the conceptual terrain is in order here, however, and will help to indicate the subsequent direction of the analysis as a whole.

The Exit Strategy: Job Shopping in the Labor Market

Libertarian theories of market economics are based upon a view of the worker as a rational agent: informed, intelligent, and actively pursuing his or her self-interest. In the labor market context, this perspective emphasizes the efforts by individual workers to seek out information on health and safety hazards and use this information when choosing occupations and employers. Rational agents avoid jobs with hazardous and otherwise undesirable working conditions. To the extent that subtle hazards are apparent only over the course of time, workers accept hazardous jobs but then quit as they become better informed. This is analogous to other individualistic and private responses to dissatisfaction in a market economy, which social scientists label "exit" strategies.

The pursuit of self-interest by individual workers has implications for the larger economic system. Employers using dangerous technologies will lack employees unless they raise wages or offer some other inducement to attract workers. These hazard pay premiums serve two functions. They partially compensate workers for the expected economic costs of eventual work-related injury or illness. The necessity for firms with risky jobs to pay higher wages also gives them incentives to invest in safety and health precautions. The costs of these investments can subsequently be recouped in the form of lower hazard pay premiums. Profit-oriented employers select the mix of safety investments and wage premiums that attracts an adequate supply of employees at the lowest total cost. In its simple form, therefore, the exit model predicts that workers will be aware of many of the hazards to which they are exposed, that quit rates will be higher in hazardous jobs than in safe jobs, and that hazardous occupations will pay higher wages than safe occupations.

There is more to be considered, however. Implicit in the hazard pay discussion is an assumption that workers are quite similar to one another in terms of skills. The reality, however, is much more complex. Workers differ remarkably in their skill levels and in the number of realistic job options they enjoy. This must be borne in mind in a discussion of hazard pay and marketplace incentives for hazard reduction. In exchange for facing health and safety risks, workers with good job possibilities demand higher wage premiums than do workers with few possibilities. To the extent that is possible, therefore, employers with hazardous technologies reorganize production processes to avoid the need for skilled workers who require high wage premiums. They often accomplish this by substituting machines and supervisory personnel for worker skills and decision-making latitude.

This shop floor reorganization has an impact on the treatment of occupational safety and health hazards by the labor market. Hazardous occupations require less formal education and offer fewer possibilities for on-the-job training and promotion than safe occupations. They are structured more rigidly and rely less upon worker motivation and creativity. Lower skill levels reduce the costs of turnover, since each employee represents less of a hiring and training investment to the employer. The combination of lower educational requirements, less on-the-job training, and higher turnover permits employers to pay lower wages in hazardous occupations than in safe occupations.

The longer-term effects of worker exit responses to work-place hazards thus produces a pattern quite different from that emerging from the simple exit model discussed earlier. Rather than paying higher wages than those paid for safe positions, jobs posing health and safety risks pay lower wages. Rather than being filled by rational agents who are well informed of the risks, hazardous jobs are often given to workers who have little formal education and who have difficulty recognizing subtle hazards. Rather than quitting at the first sight of danger, workers are often convinced that the other available jobs are equally bad and that their best option is to struggle for improved conditions in their existing positions.

The Voice Strategy: Collective Action in the Private Workplace

Several features of the labor market render exit strategies ineffective and motivate individual workers to pool their resources and seek collective solutions. First, information on health risks and methods of control is often quite technical. Labor unions are better able to gain access to and interpret this information than are individual workers. Second, toxic exposures and unsafe conditions often endanger all members of a particular work group. Workers usually cannot negotiate individually with management. Third, workers have much greater bargaining power when negotiating with management as a group than when negotiating individually. Labor unionism is analogous to other collective responses to dissatisfaction. These responses are often labeled "voice" strategies to distinguish them from the exit alternative.

Successful voice strategies to reduce workplace hazards often require the involvement of labor unions and other worker-oriented organizations. In the United States, formal union representation is typically established through an election process conducted by the National Labor Relations Board. Unions petition the NLRB to conduct an election only when they feel there exists sufficient interest within the nonunion work force to give the union a reasonable chance of winning. The voice model of worker responses to workplace hazards predicts that nonunion workers in hazardous jobs are more interested in union representation than are nonunion workers in safe jobs, that representation elections occur more frequently and are won by unions more frequently in hazardous jobs, and that the fraction of the work force that has achieved union representation is higher in hazardous than in safe sectors of the economy.

Through health and safety programs labor unions perform four essential functions. On the most basic level, they improve workers' access to information on the identity of the substances used in the production process, their toxicity, and the prevalent exposure levels. Second, through their grievance and arbitration mechanisms, unions promote procedural justice in the adjudication of health and safety disputes. In particular, unions support individual workers disciplined or discharged for refusing to perform exceptionally hazardous tasks. Third, unions negotiate with management over wages, working conditions, and other terms of employment. In response to growing worker and citizen interest in occupational health, unions have significantly increased the extent of collective bargaining concerning this topic. Working conditions vary widely from workplace to workplace, however, and rarely play central, unifying roles in collective bargaining. The heterogeneity of working conditions has encouraged unions to develop a fourth approach: joint union-management health and safety committees. These committees allow unions to be involved in health and safety matters on a daily basis and to adjust their focus of activity quickly in response to changes in working conditions.

In addition to organizing activities directed explicitly at health and safety matters, unions have significant indirect effects on working conditions. The higher wages, better fringe benefits, and strengthened job security that unions negotiate for workers in hazardous occupations enhance the overall attractiveness of these jobs. Skilled workers with many job options are more willing to accept employment in hazardous positions than they would be in the absence of union representation. If a hazardous job offers high wages, it is often because of the efforts of a labor union.

Through voice strategies and collective bargaining, therefore, workers can sometimes counteract management responses to individual exit strategies. The effectiveness of voice strategies depends, however, on the larger industrial relations environment. Recent years have been characterized by increasingly militant management resistance to labor unionism and collective bargaining. Unions have been largely unsuccessful in countering this offensive. Strike rates, union representation elections in nonunion firms, and the overall percentage of the work force that is unionized have declined rapidly. Because of these developments, the private voice strategy is becoming less effective as a means for controlling health and safety hazards in the workplace.

The Legal Strategy:
Public Guarantees for Individual Workers' Rights

In abstract legal and economic models of the labor market, employees and employers are often described as equals. Each needs the other and each bargains to his or her best advantage. This conceptual framework is embodied in the judicial doctrine of "employment at will," which interprets the employer's right to fire unwanted workers as analogous to the worker's right to quit unattractive jobs. The reality of the contemporary economy is quite different. Firms have much better access to information on health and safety hazards than do workers, and often conceal this information from their employees. Employers also possess much greater bargaining power than employees. They can use their authority under the employment-at-will doctrine to discharge the most informed and concerned workers, those most likely to lead collective voice efforts. Rather than providing labor market incentives for hazard reduction, such management-initiated exit strategies reduce pressures to improve working conditions. In this context, the abstract model of the employee and employer as equals serves as an ideological justification for a reality of inequality and coerced consent.

The inability of the exit and voice strategies to control workplace hazards effectively has produced a third alternative, the pursuit of judicial guarantees for workers' rights. This strategy tends to be individualistic in orientation, forcing employers to reinstate a discharged employee or compensate a diseased one. It is public rather than private in nature, using the courts and administrative agencies rather than market incentives. The legal strategy for controlling workplace hazards is part of a broad process of change in U.S. labor law.

The National Labor Relations Act (NLRA) of 1935 eroded the employment-at-will doctrine and legitimized a public role in upholding the private rights of workers. The NLRA facilitated the establishment of labor unions to balance the otherwise overwhelming power of employers. Since 1935, however, the principles embodied in the NLRA have gradually lost public support. Individual workers and the citizenry at large have become dissatisfied with the strategy of guaranteeing rights of individual workers indirectly, by establishing labor unions. Rather, workers and citizens have inclined toward guaranteeing workers' rights directly, through laws enforceable in the courts. Beginning most prominently with state antidiscrimination laws and the federal Civil Rights Act of 1964, a growing body of legislation has been enacted that provides direct guarantees of specified workers' rights. These public guarantees have developed in the same period in which management resistance has undermined private labor union guarantees of those rights.

Three distinct health-related areas of workers' rights have been enforced by the courts, albeit with varying degrees of success, and a fourth area is emerging. The most widely recognized right currently enjoyed by individual workers is the right to information and training concerning toxic exposures on the job. The "right to know" is now firmly established in statutes, ordinances, and regulations at the federal, state, and local levels. It can be enforced by the Occupational Safety and Health Administration, state health departments, local fire departments, emergency response programs, and the courts. The second area of workers' rights concerns due process and fairness in the adjudication of grievances. The doctrine of employment at will has been steadily eroded by court rulings that protect workers against discipline and discharge when pursuing socially desirable goals. Foremost among these "public policy exceptions" to the at-will doctrine have been discharges of workers who have demanded information on health risks or refused to perform hazardous tasks. The third area of rights concerns freedom of speech in discussing work-related problems outside the workplace. A large number of statutes and court decisions have recognized the social utility of individual "whistle-blowers" who report violations of health, safety, and environmental laws or otherwise disclose socially undesirable practices in the private sector. The Occupational Safety and Health Act, the Clean Air Act, the Clean Water Act, and other major statutes include protections for workers who report violations, and generic whistle-blower protection legislation has been considered.

While important for protecting the rights of individual workers, these developments in public law and policy have proven to be an incomplete substitute for labor unionism and collective bargaining. Partly in response to the development of union-management health and safety committees, recent initiatives have supported a fourth area of workers' rights—the right of free association. In a number of experimental projects, the Occupational Safety and Health Administration has exempted from inspection and enforcement firms that establish joint labor-management health and safety committees with specified powers. National environmental legislation has mandated the establishment of state and local committees to receive and respond to firm-specific data on toxic chemical inventories and emissions. Activists at the state level are advocating statutes that require all large firms to establish labor-management health and safety committees. These due process, whistle-blower protection, and committee structures are often conceptualized as components of the individual worker's "right to act" to control workplace hazards, a direct extension of his or her "right to know" about exposure to those hazards.

The Regulatory Strategy: Political Mobilization for Public Health

Governmental right-to-know and right-to-act policies are beset by two severe limitations. First, information on the extent of risk posed by working conditions is often unavailable or unreliable. Labor unions are better situated than individual workers to obtain and interpret such information, but still face major barriers. Right-to-know statutes and standards have required employers to divulge exposure and health effects data but do not require them to generate such data in the first place. Second, the ability of workers to respond to health and safety information depends upon their individual job options and the larger industrial relations climate. Exit opportunities are meager for the unskilled and disadvantaged workers who disproportionately fill hazardous occupations. Voice opportunities are limited for workers facing aggressive employers in an increasingly nonunion economy. Legal opportunities are better suited for compensating aggrieved individuals than for changing the structural causes of occupational injuries and illnesses. There is no guarantee that the pursuit of these exit, voice, and legal initiatives by workers will result in socially acceptable control of toxic substances and unsafe conditions.

The weaknesses of the exit, voice, and legal strategies have generated support for the fourth alternative: direct regulation of workplace hazards by governmental agencies. Collective and public in orientation, the regulatory strategy provides a mechanism for the development of new data on workplace risks and for the creation and enforcement of standards limiting worker exposures. Embodied principally in the Occupational Safety and Health Act of 1970, the regulatory strategy for controlling toxic exposures in the workplace is broadly similar to regulatory strategies for ensuring consumer product safety and environmental protection. The 1970 act established an agency within the Department of Health and Human Services to research hazards and recommend standards and another agency within the Department of Labor to promulgate and enforce standards. These institutions have the authority to conduct or commission evaluations of the health effects of particular substances and the economic costs of control technologies. They have the power to enforce stringent standards throughout most sectors of private industry. Their efforts cover all strata of the work force, including unskilled and nonunion workers. Individual workers, labor unions, and public interest groups have pursued the regulatory strategy by supporting new standards and reporting violations of existing ones.

While eluding some of the most effective forms of management resistance of workplace health and safety efforts, the regulatory strategy elicits its own very potent industry opposition. During periods of liberal dominance, industry contests standards and citations in the courts. During periods of conservative dominance, industry opposes regulation from within the executive sector of government. Depending upon the political climate, industry has favored outright elimination of the regulatory agencies, maintenance of the agency structures without meaningful activity, and a policy of moderate promulgation and enforcement of standards to forestall demands for vigorous action. The changing tides of political power create ebbs and flows in the effectiveness of the regulatory strategy.

Evaluating Alternative Strategies

This book uses a wide range of economic, political, and legal data to analyze and evaluate the four basic strategies pursued by workers to control exposure to toxic substances and unsafe conditions. The choice between individual exit and collective voice strategies is presented in chapter 2, which documents worker perceptions of hazard, quit intentions and quits, prounion sentiment among nonunion workers, the incidence and outcome of union representation elections, and the extent of unionization in hazardous and safe sectors of the economy. Given the significant changes in industrial relations over the past thirty years, an important part of this analysis concerns trends in these worker strategies, particularly those involving labor unions.

The voice strategy is pursued in the following two chapters. Chapter 3 highlights the most important features of labor union health and safety activities and documents the spread of these activities across unionized firms from the late 1950s to the late 1980s. The effects of worker voice and management resistance on the performance of the economy is documented in chapter 4. Statistical data on worker dissatisfaction and absenteeism, employer discharges of insubordinate employees, authorized and wildcat strikes, labor productivity, and corporate profits paint a powerful picture of the social costs of hazard-related industrial conflict.

Chapters 5 and 6 deal with the implications of worker and management initiatives for the structure of jobs and the mix of workers in hazardous occupations. The de-skilling of hazardous jobs is documented at length in chapter 5, with data on educational requirements, on-the-job training and promotion possibilities, worker autonomy and decision-making authority, employment security, and wages. Hazardous jobs pay wages slightly above those paid in safe jobs that have similar skill requirements. But skill requirements, and therefore wages, are generally lower in hazardous jobs than in safe employments. Inequality in the value of jobs presupposes inequality in access to skills and training. Only in societies where the working class is deeply divided along racial or other lines is there a stratum of disadvantaged workers willing to accept jobs that are both hazardous and low-paying.

Chapter 6 documents the concentration of Hispanic and black workers in hazardous jobs and links this to the overall logic of labor market competition.

The book's emphasis then shifts from the private to the public arena, focusing on legal and regulatory strategies for controlling occupational hazards. Chapter 7 treats the politics and legal development of the right-to-know movement, the most successful worker initiative in recent years. The origin of community disclosure campaigns in labor union efforts and the feedback loop from the legislative to the workplace arena highlight the close interdependence between public and private efforts in occupational health. The extension of the right-to-know principles to a broader doctrine of the worker's right to act is studied in chapter 8 within the context of the recent changes in the industrial relations system. The regulatory strategy is analyzed in chapter 9, which follows the tortuous and heavily conflictual history of standards setting by the Occupational Safety and Health Administration.

The final chapter returns to the four-part classification matrix and compares the strengths and weaknesses of the exit, voice, legal, and regulatory strategies for controlling occupational hazards. Each alternative is evaluated first in terms of the economic costs it imposes in reducing risks. More important, the four strategies are then judged on the basis of their compatibility with philosophical values concerning the appropriate distribution of risks and the appropriate mechanisms for controlling risks in a market economy and democratic polity.

2

Fight or Flight?

Health and safety hazards are an important dimension of job quality, but one about which there is often great uncertainty. Workers may be quite ignorant as to the risks presented by any particular job at the time the job is offered. Once they accept particular jobs, however, workers have the opportunity to learn more about the hazards posed to their well-being. This is true not only for risks of relatively frequent events, such as injuries and acute illnesses, but also for some subtle diseases, as shown by the DBCP case.

As workers' understanding of job hazards improves, some find that conditions are significantly more dangerous than they had initially envisaged. This discovery is analogous to a consumer's realization that the quality of the product he or she is used to buying has deteriorated. The response may be the same in both cases. Consumers who learn about deterioration in quality sometimes switch brands; workers who learn about health and safety hazards sometimes switch jobs.[1] The immediate effect of the quit is to remove the worker from the hazard. The hazardous job remains, however, and the firm must find another worker to fill it. The process of screening, hiring, and training a replacement worker may be quite costly. These costs must be taken into account when the firm decides how much to invest in health and safety improvements. Worker quits raise the cost of unsafe working conditions and give the firm incentives to improve conditions, since quit rates will be lower in safer jobs. Some conservatives have pointed to this process of hazard-related quits as an explanation of how unregulated labor markets might reduce occupational injuries and illnesses without governmental intervention.[2]

The notion that workers learn about the hazards they face is plausible. While ignorance and apathy are to be found in the workplace as they are elsewhere, they can hardly be the worker's dominant psychological response. But there are clear limits to worker turnover. The willingness of a worker to quit his or her job based on new information about a health or safety hazard depends on the worker's estimate of the chances of finding a better job elsewhere. It does not make sense to quit one hazardous job only to end up in another one. It makes even less sense to quit a job you have, no matter what the working conditions, only to end up unemployed and dependent on the meager generosity of the welfare system.

The likelihood that a worker recognizing a new health and safety hazard will pause before quitting is increased by the fact that the desirability of one's job tends to increase the longer one has it. Over time, workers often gain on-the-job training that raises their productivity in their current job but would be of little value in any other firm. Their employer is likely to reward this higher productivity with wage increases; no such increases would be obtained if the worker quit and switched firms. Not only does productivity increase with job tenure, but workers often gain seniority rights. "First come, first served" is a common principle governing personnel policy inside firms. These productivity and seniority issues explain why most of the quitting that occurs in the U.S. economy is done by junior employees with only short job tenure. The effects of productivity and seniority are particularly relevant to the topic at hand, for even while the worker's understanding of occupational health and safety hazards is improving, he or she is gaining tenure-related rights that make it distasteful to quit.

If quitting is not a viable option, workers are likely to seek ways to reduce workplace health and safety risks without switching jobs. In some cases, merely raising the issue with management will bring improvements. In cases where reductions in health and safety hazards require substantial investments of time and money, however, management is unlikely to respond favorably to worker requests. Individuals confronted with this situation may seek to join fellow workers in pressuring management. Spontaneous associations of workers may spring up around particular grievances. In order for these collective efforts to succeed, however, they may need formal union representation. In the United States, this is usually done by petitioning the National Labor Relations Board for a secret ballot election. The employees then vote in favor of or against the labor union that seeks to represent them in negotiations with management.

Workers thus must choose between two workplace strategies. Together with coworkers, they can pressure management to install protective equipment, change work processes, or otherwise act directly to make the workplace a safer and healthier place. As individuals, they can quit and search for better working conditions elsewhere. Social scientists distinguish between voice and exit responses to dissatisfaction. Biologists use more evocative language: when threatened, people must choose between "fight" and "flight."

Worker Perceptions of Workplace Hazards: Risk of Injury and Acute Illness

In order to evaluate the accuracy of worker perceptions of occupational hazards, we require a standard of comparison. Many illnesses can be caused by both occupational and nonoccupational factors; thus it is difficult to develop estimates of the rates of illness attributable directly to workplace exposures. The statistical problem is much less severe for work-related injuries and acute illnesses such as dermatitis. Data on injuries and acute illnesses are usually categorized by the industry rather than by the occupation of the affected workers. Fortunately, occupational data can be obtained from the mandatory reporting system in the state of California. Each year the state publishes the number of acute illnesses, strains and sprains, cuts and punctures, bone fractures, and other categories of injuries for each occupation. When linked with employment data, these figures can be used to compute rates of disabling injuries and acute illnesses for each occupation.[3]

The 1986 rates of disabling injuries and acute illnesses for each major occupational group in California are shown in table 2. Disabling injuries and illnesses are defined in the California reporting system as events requiring at least one full day lost from work, and are here presented in terms of annual events per 1,000 workers. The rate of injuries and illnesses for all occupations combined, 34.5 per 1,000, means that an average of 3½% of California workers suffer a disabling injury or acute illness each year. These data do not capture the health effects of chronic exposure to toxic substances, since events such as cancer often occur long after the initial exposure and are typically not recognized or reported as work-related.

Table 2
*Rates of Disabling Injuries and Acute Illnesses
per 1,000 Workers by Occupation in California, 1986*

	Total Injuries, Illnesses	*Strains, Sprains*	*Cuts, Punctures*	*Bone Fractures*	*Acute Illnesses*
All occupations	34.5	14.9	4.6	3.5	2.6
White-collar workers	12.7	5.9	0.9	1.3	1.6
Service workers	56.5	21.8	7.0	3.7	4.6
Craft workers	57.3	19.5	9.3	5.9	2.5
Operatives	55.8	18.0	5.1	4.5	2.4
Laborers	144.6	64.9	20.7	14.9	5.7

The wide variation in injury and illness rates across occupations is striking. While 13 workers per 1,000 employed in white-collar occupations suffer an injury or illness each year, 145 workers per 1,000 employed in laborer occupations are disabled. Service workers, craft workers, and operatives are at an intermediate level of risk, with approximately 56 per 1,000 suffering an injury or illness. By far the most common type of injury is strains and sprains, accounting for over 40% of the total. Acute illnesses account for approximately 7.5% of the total. It is interesting to note that the range across occupations for acute illnesses is narrower than that for injuries.

In seeking to understand worker responses to these safety and health risks, an obvious first step is to examine the extent that workers perceive their jobs as hazardous. No matter what the true level of risk posed by working conditions, we would not expect to observe exit or voice strategies unless workers recognize those hazards. Three national surveys conducted over the past two decades have queried workers concerning their exposure to health and safety hazards on the job. The 1977 Quality of Employment Survey (QES), conducted by the University of Michigan, asked 1,515 workers a large number of questions concerning the characteristics of their jobs, including thirteen questions on exposure to different types of health and safety hazards.[4] The 1978 and 1980 National Longitudinal Surveys (NLS), conducted by Ohio State University, asked two questions relating to health and safety hazards.[5] These questions were posed to men in the 1978 survey and to women in the 1980 survey. The two surveys can be combined to provide a relatively balanced portrait of the U.S. work force. The combined NLS had 4,538 respondents but was limited to workers between the ages of 26 and 39. The 1984 Louis Harris survey (AFL), funded by the AFL-CIO labor union federation, included 1,405 workers and asked one question concerning exposure to health and safety hazards.[6] For present purposes, respondents to these three surveys are considered to perceive their jobs as hazardous if they report substantial exposures. Workers who report only minor levels of exposure are considered to perceive their jobs as safe.

The percentages of workers responding to the QES, NLS, and AFL surveys who report that their jobs entail serious risks to either health or safety are provided in table 3. It is significant that a large percentage of both men and women report hazards. Examining all occupations together, approximately 40% of the men and 30% of the women report at least one serious hazard. These numbers indicate above all else that workers are not wholly ignorant of the health and safety hazards they face on the job.

The survey respondents are also divided in table 3 into five major occupational categories, and the percentages of men and women in each category that report serious hazard exposures are documented. Approximately one-fourth of white-collar workers report the presence of workplace hazards; the percentages are much higher for service and blue-collar occupations. Among men, one-half or more of blue-collar workers report serious hazards; among women, the range is from one-third to over one-half.

Table 3
*Percentage of Workers Reporting Serious
Health and Safety Hazards on the Job, 1977–1984*

	Men			Women		
	1977 QES	1978 NLS	1984 AFL	1977 QES	1980 NLS	1984 AFL
All occupations	42.3	36.4	45.9	30.7	25.0	32.1
White-collar workers	27.1	21.1	29.8	24.8	21.0	25.7
Service workers	61.8	42.2	43.3	31.3	33.3	42.0
Craft workers	47.5	59.6	62.8	25.0	35.9	53.7
Operatives	65.8	61.3	65.2	54.3	42.3	50.0
Laborers	53.3	66.1	65.2	60.0	49.6	50.0

It is interesting to compare the injury and illness rates in table 2 with the percentages of workers reporting exposure to hazards in table 3. The rates in table 2 are presented in terms of number of events per year per 1,000 workers, but approximate the percentage of workers that are injured or become ill over the course of a decade (i.e., events per ten-year period per 100 workers). The QES, NLS, and AFL survey respondents were asked about exposure to hazards, not about the likelihood of becoming injured or ill within one calendar year. If we choose to interpret the figures in table 3 as the respondents' estimate of the likelihood of becoming injured or ill over the course of ten years' employment, then the numbers in the two tables can be compared directly. Although somewhat arbitrary, this assumption is not implausible as an interpretation of the meaning of worker hazard perceptions. The ten-year rate of injuries and acute illnesses for all California occupations in table 2, 35%, is within the range of the percentages of men and women who report hazard exposures, 25–46%. These figures are also quite close to the national rate of disabling work-related injuries and acute illnesses, published by the U.S. Bureau of Labor Statistics (BLS) and based on an annual survey of establishments. The national rate of injuries and illnesses requiring at least one day lost from work ranged from a low of 33 per 1,000 in 1975 to 38 per 1,000 in 1987, with a peak of 43 per 1,000 in 1979.[7]

It is also useful to compare the range of injury rates and worker hazard perceptions across occupations. While the objective and subjective measures of hazard are fairly close for service workers, craft workers, and operatives, they diverge significantly for the groups at the two ends of the risk spectrum. While about one-fourth of white-collar workers report serious hazard exposures, only half that many suffer a disabling injury or acute illness over a ten-year period. On the other hand, the ten-year rate of injuries and illnesses for laborers is almost three times as high as the percentage of laborers reporting hazard exposures. The high prevalence of reported exposures among white-collar workers, compared to their injury and illness rate, may be due partly to their concern for longer-term health hazards whose effects are not captured in official statistics. The fact that one-third to one-half of laborers report no significant health and safety hazards, despite the high rates of disabling injuries and illnesses in that occupation, may reflect ignorance or apathy due to low levels of education and few alternative job options.

Worker Perceptions of Workplace Hazards: Risks of Cancer

While workers may be reasonably familiar with workplace risks of injury and acute illness, they are probably much less sure of their risk of illnesses such as cancer, loss of lung function, or neurological damage. These chronic medical problems are of great importance, however, and it is impossible to assess the potential effectiveness of worker exit and voice strategies without some insight into workers' abilities to recognize these more subtle dangers. Unfortunately, only scant data are available on occupational disease. The National Institute for Occupational Safety and Health has developed indexes of exposure to chemical hazards based on toxicological and exposure data. When linked to surveys that query workers concerning occupational exposure to dangerous chemicals and unhealthy working conditions, the NIOSH risk index can provide some insights into the validity of worker perceptions of chronic health hazards.

The NIOSH index is based on toxicological data from the Registry of Toxic Effects of Chemical Substances (RTECS). The registry is a compilation of published toxicological data on each of a large number of chemicals, derived from a comprehensive review of the scientific literature.[8] The majority of the toxic effects reported in the registry are derived from laboratory studies using animals. Information on worker exposure to chemicals on the RTECS list can be obtained from the 1972–74 National Occupational Health Survey (NOHS), conducted by NIOSH to ascertain the type of exposures occurring in the U.S. economy. Specially trained engineers toured 5,000 facilities in 67 metropolitan areas and recorded worker exposures to each chemical, the extent to which the exposure was controlled, and whether the exposure was full-time or part-time for the workers. The 5,000 facilities were selected to be representative of the entire nonagricultural business sector. The RTECS and NOHS data were combined to create an index for each of 231 occupations.[9] The index multiplies NOHS data on the fractions of employees in each occupation exposed to each chemical with RTECS data on the carcinogenicity of each chemical. This permits a ranking of occupations in terms of exposure to carcinogens; it cannot, however, be interpreted as an estimate of the fraction of employees who will actually get cancer. For purposes of illustration, the 20 occupations with the highest cancer indexes are presented in table 4.

In order to ascertain whether workers in occupations with high NIOSH cancer indexes report exposure to health hazards, the cancer index was linked to worker data from the 1977 Quality of Employment Survey and 1978 and 1980 National Longitudinal Surveys.[10] These two surveys queried workers concerning their perceptions of health hazard exposures on the job. The QES included thirteen questions concerning different types of health and safety risks. None of the questions focused explicitly on cancer risks. One question, however, queried workers as to whether or not they face exposure to "dangerous chemicals." Seven percent of the QES workers reported "sizeable" or "great" exposures of this type. The NLS respondents were asked two health and safety questions, one concerning exposure to "dangerous" working conditions and the other concerning exposure to "unhealthy conditions." Twenty-two percent of the NLS workers reported substantial exposure to "unhealthy conditions." The NLS measure of worker-perceived health hazard is thus broader than its counterpart in the QES.

The percentages of QES and NLS workers in occupations with high and low NIOSH cancer indexes who report serious exposures to dangerous chemicals and unhealthy conditions are provided in table 5.[11] These percentages are adjusted for

Table 4
Occupations with Greatest Exposure to Carcinogens
(Based on the NIOSH Cancer Index)

Occupation	Number of Carcinogens	Cancer Index
Agriculture and biological technicians	17	.170
Biological scientists	14	.125
Clinical laboratory technologists and technicians	22	.120
Chemists	58	.095
Mixing operatives	60	.088
Hairdressers and cosmetologists	2	.084
Housekeepers, exc. private household	5	.064
Millwrights	17	.061
Pharmacists	6	.058
Chemical technicians	43	.058
Painters, construction and maintenance workers	14	.057
Aircraft mechanics	17	.056
Pattern and model makers	13	.053
Machinists	22	.045
Brick masons and stone masons	5	.044
Air conditioning, heating, and refrigeration mechanics	11	.044
Miscellaneous mechanics and repairmen	13	.042
Tool and die makers	20	.042
Jewelers and watchmakers	3	.040
Boilermakers	7	.037

the race, sex, age, and educational level of individual workers, since such factors might influence the accuracy of worker hazard perceptions. The association between the cancer index and worker perceptions of exposure is striking. QES workers employed in occupations with low cancer indexes are highly unlikely to report the presence of dangerous chemicals, but 13% of those in high-risk occupations reported significant or

Table 5
Percentage of Workers Reporting Hazardous Chemical
Exposures and Unhealthy Working Conditions,
According to Cancer Risk Faced

	High Cancer-Risk Occupations	*Low Cancer-Risk Occupations*
Workers reporting "hazardous chemicals" (1977 QES)	12.8	0.0
Workers reporting "unhealthy conditions" (1978–80 NLS)	32.5	4.9

great exposures. Five percent of NLS workers in occupations
with low cancer indexes reported unhealthy conditions, while
almost one-third of those in occupations with high indexes reported unhealthy conditions.

The association between cancer risks and worker perceptions can be interpreted as a glass half full or a glass half
empty. On the one hand, a worker is more likely to report
health hazards if employed in an occupation with a high cancer index. On the other hand, substantially less than half of
the workers in occupations with the highest cancer indexes
considered themselves at significant risk. Whether this implies that workers underestimate the hazards they face depends on the absolute level of cancer risk implied by high values on the NIOSH index. It may be that only small minorities
of workers in these occupations are at high risk of suffering
from the illness. The other possible explanation, however, is
that many workers who face serious risk of occupational cancer do not recognize that fact.

The Exit Strategy: Quit Intentions and Quits

The exit model of worker responses to workplace hazards focuses on the propensity of workers to quit their jobs and

search for better working conditions elsewhere. Several studies based on data collected during the late 1960s and early 1970s found a positive association between the degree of hazard posed by a worker's job and the likelihood that the worker would express an intention to quit or actually would quit the job.[12] The late 1960s and early 1970s were a unique period in postwar American history during which business boomed and job opportunities abounded for workers. The combination of high government demand for goods and services related to the Vietnam War and high consumer demand related to rising incomes created a labor market of unequaled opportunity for even the most disadvantaged workers. Workers responded to this labor market bonanza by switching jobs frequently in search of the best combination of wages and working conditions. Quit rates soared.

This golden age was apparently too good to last. The sharp recession of 1974–75 ended the euphoria, and the second half of the decade was characterized by sluggish growth in productivity and consumer incomes. The early 1980s witnessed the most dramatic drop in output since the Great Depression of the 1930s, and unemployment rates rose to double-digit levels for the first time in decades. Starting in 1983, the economy began a strong recovery in terms of overall output and employment. For some industries, however, especially those faced by rising competition from imported goods, no such recovery occurred. Workers reacted cautiously to the economic uncertainties of these times. Hopping from job to job no longer seemed prudent when a hop out of one job did not necessarily permit a hop into another. It is imperative, therefore, to examine how workers responded to occupational safety and health hazards in the period since the early data were collected.

In studying the association between hazard exposures and quits, it is necessary to use many different sources of information in order to obtain the broadest possible view of the labor market. The surveys employed earlier all contain measures of worker turnover. The QES and AFL surveys were conducted only one time and thus cannot shed light directly on whether exposure to workplace hazards at one point in time is linked to worker quits in a subsequent period. The surveys did, however, query respondents as to whether they intended to quit their jobs over the next year.[13] When linked to measures of hazard exposure, these measures of quit intentions provide initial insights into worker exit responses to workplace hazards.

The NLS differs from the QES and AFL surveys because it reinterviews respondents every two years. In each round of interviews respondents are asked whether they quit their job since the previous interview. The answers to these questions in the 1980 men's NLS and the 1982 women's NLS can be compared with the answers to the hazard exposure questions from the 1978 men's and 1980 women's surveys. The NLS data can thus directly answer the question of whether exposure to workplace hazards in one year increases the likelihood that a worker will quit over the following two years.

Two sources of statistical data on worker turnover exist aside from the QES, AFL, and NLS surveys. The Panel Study of Income Dynamics (PSID) is a longitudinal survey conducted by the University of Michigan that is similar in many respects to the NLS. It annually reinterviews approximately 6,000 individuals, of which 3,500 to 4,500 are employed and answer all relevant questions in any given year. The PSID queries respondents as to quits between interview periods and thus provides measures of turnover similar to those supplied by the NLS. The 1976–78 and 1985–87 years of the survey are used here. Unfortunately, the PSID does not contain questions concerning worker perceptions of hazard. It does, however, report the industry in which each respondent is employed. This industry information can be linked with national data on annual rates of disabling injuries and acute illnesses to determine whether workers in risky industries are more likely to quit their jobs than workers in safe industries. Analogous insights can be obtained from a 1977 U.S. Bureau of Labor Statistics survey of manufacturing establishments. The BLS data use manufacturing industries rather than individual workers as the unit of analysis.

In examining the determinants of worker quits, one must account for factors other than the level of hazard to health and safety. Job characteristics such as wage rates, training and promotion possibilities, and the threat of layoff are very likely to influence the worker's decision to quit. It stands to reason that workers are less likely to quit good jobs than bad jobs. The state of the labor market, as regards opportunities for new job openings, is another important determinant. Unemployment rates for the nation as a whole vary from year to year and have tended to be higher in the years since 1975 than in prior years. Economic conditions also vary according to the geographical area in which the worker lives. The economic recessions and recoveries of the past decades have affected different cities, states, and regions quite differently. Finally, characteristics of the workers themselves are associated with the likelihood that they will quit their jobs in any year. Younger workers are more prone to quit than are older workers, since they are more likely to return to school and test different careers before making a final choice. Junior workers are more likely to quit than senior workers because they have not yet gained tenure-related benefits. Demographic characteristics such as race, sex, and education level might play a role in turnover patterns if different demographic groups have different degrees of attachment to the labor force.

Rates of reported quit intentions and actual quits for workers in safe and hazardous jobs are supplied in table 6. These figures are statistically adjusted for differences among workers and jobs with reference to the factors discussed above. Adjusted rates of quit intentions and quits should be interpreted as the rates that would be observed in hazardous and safe jobs if those jobs were identical except for the dangers they pose and if the workers employed there were identical in terms of demographic characteristics.[14]

The percentages of QES and AFL workers in the first two rows of the table represent the workers in hazardous and safe

Table 6
Percentage of Workers in Hazardous and Safe Jobs Intending
to Quit or Actually Quitting, 1976–1987

	Men		Women	
	Hazardous Jobs	Safe Jobs	Hazardous Jobs	Safe Jobs
Intending to quit				
1977 QES	37.5	26.6	46.5	32.9
1984 AFL	22.4	19.9	16.9	13.8
Actually quit				
1977 BLS	23.4	17.6	23.4	17.6
1978–82 NLS	12.0	15.5	19.2	21.1
1976–79 PSID	10.4	9.7	11.7	19.1
1985–87 PSID	11.4	10.8	19.1	12.9

jobs who reported plans to quit their jobs over the next year. For these data, hazard is defined in terms of the worker's subjective perception of exposure to serious risk of any occupational injury or illness. Workers who perceive their jobs as hazardous are more likely than workers not perceiving hazard to report intentions to quit; this pattern is consistent with the exit theory of worker responses to hazard. The strength of the association is much stronger in the QES than in the later survey, however. While male and female QES respondents in hazardous jobs are approximately 40% more likely to express quit intentions than are respondents in safe jobs, the differential declines to 13% for men and 22% for women in the 1984 AFL survey.

The 1977 rates of quits experienced by manufacturing firms with high and low rates of injuries, respectively, are given in the third row of the table. Here the perspective is that of the firm or the industry, rather than that of the individual worker. Turnover is measured in terms of the number of quits per 100 employees per year. Industries are categorized as hazardous or safe according to whether their rate of disabling injuries and acute illnesses in 1977 was above or below the average for all manufacturing industries in that year. These quit rates are statistically adjusted for industry differences in wages and work force characteristics such as age, race, sex, education level, and employment tenure. Consistent with the data on quit intentions in the QES and AFL, quit rates are significantly higher in hazardous industries than in safe industries.

While the association between perceived exposures and quit intentions for QES and AFL workers and between injury and quit rates for manufacturing firms is supportive of the exit theory, the data are quite limited. Quit intentions are not the same as actual quits, and one year's experience in the manufacturing sector is not necessarily representative of other years in other sectors. The best sources of data on worker turnover are the NLS and PSID surveys, which contain information on actual quit behavior for workers in all sectors of the economy over an extended period of years.

The percentages of workers who quit hazardous and safe jobs over the 1976–87 period, shown in the fourth, fifth, and sixth rows of table 6, have been statistically adjusted to account for other causes of worker turnover. Workplace hazard has no consistent effect on worker quits, regardless of whether hazard is measured in terms of subjective worker perceptions, as in the NLS, or in terms of official injury rates, as in the PSID. Quit rates are actually higher in safe jobs than in hazardous jobs for male and female workers in the NLS and for female workers in the 1976–79 PSID. Quit rates are significantly higher in hazardous jobs as compared to safe jobs only among female workers in the 1985–87 PSID.

What can we conclude from this mix of findings? The exit theory of worker response to workplace hazards emerges substantially weakened, compared to the position it enjoyed based on the earlier studies, which used data from 1969 through 1975. While quit intentions among QES and AFL survey respondents and quit rates in manufacturing industries were positively associated with hazard levels, individual quit probabilities among PSID and NLS survey respondents were often lower in hazardous than in safe employments.

The Voice Strategy:
Union Elections and Representation

Workers need not quit their jobs once they discover the hazards there; they can join with coworkers and strive to improve conditions. Voice strategies of this type do not necessarily require the presence of independent worker organizations such as labor unions. In practice, however, labor unions often are of great value in helping workers evaluate their working conditions and in coordinating efforts to control hazards. The uncovering of the DBCP hazard, for example, resulted from the efforts of the union representing the production workers at Occidental Chemical.

If unions provide meaningful support for health and safety efforts, then one would expect workers facing such hazards to seek union representation more frequently than workers not at comparable risk. In marked contrast to the exit strategy embodied in quit decisions, however, the voice strategy does not depend solely on decisions by individuals. A labor union must petition the National Labor Relations Board to conduct a representation election, and then campaign among the work force to obtain a majority of the votes. Management will generally respond with its own campaign to convince employees to reject union representation. Even if an election is won by the union, moreover, there is no guarantee that union representation will be achieved. Despite their legal obligation to bargain in good faith, many employers refuse to negotiate with unions who win representation elections. More than one-third of all elections won by unions fail to produce a stable union-management relationship.[15]

Four discrete facets of worker voice responses to workplace hazard need to be analyzed. First, are nonunion workers facing occupational safety and health risks more interested in union representation than nonunion workers who do not face such risks? Second, do union representation elections occur more frequently in hazardous than in safe industries? Third, what is the outcome of the union representation elections that do occur? Finally, what is the trend in the percentage of workers represented by labor unions in hazardous and safe industries?

Worker Desire for Union Representation

The QES, NLS, and AFL surveys contain information on worker attitudes toward labor unions. In all three surveys, respondents were asked whether they would vote in favor of union representation, if an election were to be held in their workplace.

The percentages of nonunion QES, NLS, and AFL respondents in hazardous and safe jobs, respectively, who expressed a willingness to vote for union representation are presented in table 7.[16] These percentages are statistically adjusted for job characteristics such as wages, training programs, promotion possibilities, and layoff threats and for worker characteristics such as race, sex, age, job tenure, and education. They are also adjusted for the region in which the worker resides and for whether the worker lives in an urban or rural area, since geographic differences are often associated with cultural factors that influence attitudes toward unions. Union strength is much lower in the southeastern United States than elsewhere, for example, due in part to geographical differences in worker attitudes. The measure of working conditions used here is based on the worker's perceptions of exposure to any health or safety hazard.

The figures in table 7 provide strong support for the voice theory of worker responses to hazard. Nonunion workers in all three surveys are substantially more likely to express a willingness to vote prounion if they perceive their jobs as hazardous than if they perceive their jobs as safe. While 21–28% of men in safe jobs are prounion, 32–39% of men in hazardous jobs express prounion sentiment. The hazard-related differ-

Table 7

*Percentage of Nonunion Workers in Hazardous and Safe Jobs
Desiring Union Representation, 1977–1984*

	Men		Women	
	Hazardous Jobs	Safe Jobs	Hazardous Jobs	Safe Jobs
1977 QES	39.1	23.2	52.0	36.6
1978–80 NLS	33.0	28.0	44.0	31.9
1984 AFL	32.3	20.6	40.3	30.6

ence is even more pronounced among women workers. While
31–37% of women in safe jobs state they would vote in favor
of union representation, 40–52% of women in hazardous jobs
report such intentions. It is important to note, however, that
the percentage expressing a willingness to vote in favor of
union representation declined among workers of both sexes in
hazardous jobs as well as among those in safe jobs over the
1977–84 period. While 39% of nonunion men and 52% of nonunion women in hazardous jobs expressed prounion sentiment in 1977, only 32% of men and 40% of women did so in
1984. Only a minority of unorganized workers who perceive a
serious work-related threat to their health or safety see union
representation as the solution to their problem.

Exit and Voice Responses to Cancer Risks

The analysis of worker exit and voice strategies must be extended to cover subtle long-term health hazards. For this purpose, the NIOSH cancer index can be used in conjunction
with the QES and NLS data. The percentages of workers in
occupations with high and low cancer indexes who actually
quit or report quit intentions and who report a desire for
union representation can be found in table 8. In addition to

Table 8
Percentage of Workers Who Quit or Express Prounion
Sentiment in Occupations with Different Risks of Cancer

	High Cancer Index Occu- pations	Low Cancer Index Occu- pations	Workers Reporting Exposure	Workers Reporting No Exposure
Workers quitting or intending to quit				
1977 QES	33.6	37.6	34.3	33.4
1978–80 NLS	19.8	14.4	17.0	17.6
Nonunion workers desiring union representation				
1977 QES	37.6	31.8	50.0	30.0
1978–80 NLS	34.2	27.5	40.3	31.6

the NIOSH cancer index, the subjective worker perceptions of exposure to "dangerous chemicals" and "unhealthy conditions" are used to examine worker responses to perceived health hazards. The figures on quits, quit intentions, and desire for union representation are statistically adjusted for job, worker, and labor market influences.

The association between occupational exposure to chemical carcinogens and worker quit intentions and quits, presented in the first two rows of table 8, offers no consistent support for the exit theory of worker responses to hazard. The association between quit intentions, quits, and worker perceptions of exposure to dangerous chemicals and unhealthy conditions is also inconsistent. For some surveys and measures of health hazard, workers at increased risk are more likely to quit than are workers at decreased risk, while in other cases they are less likely to quit. In contrast, the voice theory receives consistent support from these data. Adjusted percentages of QES and NLS respondents who are not unionized but who would vote in favor of union representation, were a representation election to be held, are supplied in the third and fourth rows of the table. Workers in occupations with high cancer indexes are 18–24% more likely than workers in occupations with low cancer indexes to report a willingness to vote for union representation. QES and NLS workers reporting serious exposures to hazardous chemicals and unhealthy conditions are 67% and 28%, respectively, more likely to report prounion sentiments than workers not reporting those hazards. As in the case of exposure to risks of injury and acute illness, however, at most half of the workers reporting exposure to dangerous chemicals and unhealthy conditions view union representation as the solution to their problem.

The Incidence and Outcome of Union Representation Elections

Desiring union representation is not the same as obtaining it. Nonunion employers often wage vigorous campaigns prior to union representation elections to convince their employees to reject collective bargaining. The legality of the tactics used during these campaigns has been the subject of intense controversy; prounion workers are often fired or otherwise discriminated against. For present purposes it is important to establish whether or not employee interest in unionization is sufficiently strong to overcome management resistance.

Two elements enter the question of whether workers gain union representation. First, there must be sufficient interest among the workers for a labor union to invest the substantial time and money required to mount a serious campaign. If the union is skeptical of its eventual chances for success, it will not petition the National Labor Relations Board to conduct an election. Second, a majority of the workers must vote in favor of union representation once an election has been successfully petitioned.

The NLRB collects data on every representation election it supervises, including information on the number of workers voting, the percentage voting prounion, and the final legal adjudication. The incidence rates of union representation elections in 1977, 1983, and 1987 according to the extent of injury and acute illness risk in the industry are portrayed in table 9. The incidence rates are calculated in terms of elections per 100,000 nonunionized employees in the industry, since workers already represented by unions typically do not vote in these elections. Individual industries are grouped together according to whether their rate of disabling injuries and acute illnesses in each year is high, medium, or low when compared with the rates for all industries.

The range of incidence rates is consistent with the worker survey data presented earlier and provides striking support for the notion that workers exposed to hazards often seek union representation as one means of improving their situation. In 1977 the rate of representation elections was six times higher in very hazardous industries than in safe industries. It was four times higher in moderately hazardous industries than in safe industries. Representation elections were also more frequent in hazardous than in safe industries in 1983 and 1987, but these differences are narrower. The most significant trend evidenced by the data in table 9, however, is the steep decline in the incidence of union representation elections since 1977. The 1987 election rate in the most hazardous industries was only 38% of the 1977 rate in those same industries. This change indicates that collective bargaining has become less available as a means for dealing with work-related hazards.

Table 9

Union Representation Elections per 100,000 Nonunion Workers in Hazardous and Safe Industries, 1977–1987

	1977	1983	1987
Most hazardous industries	15.6	11.7	6.0
Moderately hazardous industries	10.8	5.6	6.7
Least hazardous industries	2.6	2.4	2.8

Declines in the rate at which representation elections occur could in principle be offset by increases in the rate of success enjoyed by unions in those elections that are held. Trends in the percentages of nonunion workers voting prounion and in the rate of union victory in representation elections are illustrated in table 10. While union success rates increased slightly over the 1977–87 decade, the gain was not sufficient to offset the membership losses due to the decline in the incidence of elections. Unions consistently won a larger percentage of elections in industries with high injury rates than in industries with low injury rates. Even so, however, they won only about half of the ever-dwindling number of elections.

The figures in table 10 reflect differences in election outcomes according to the level of hazard but are not adjusted for other differences among industries and firms that influence election outcomes. Needless to say, characteristics of the workers, employers, and labor unions involved can all be expected to influence the fraction of votes won by the union and the likelihood that the union will be officially certified as the election winner by the NLRB. To examine whether the inclusion of other factors would substantially alter the conclusions

Table 10
Percentage of Workers Voting Prounion and Representation Elections Won by Unions in Hazardous and Safe Industries, 1977–1987

	Workers Voting Prounion			Elections Won by Unions		
	1977	1983	1987	1977	1983	1987
Most hazardous industries	51.1	57.1	54.8	44.8	54.4	50.4
Moderately hazardous industries	50.3	51.9	52.5	43.5	45.1	51.3
Least hazardous industries	49.5	46.0	55.0	41.0	34.6	48.5

derived from the data provided in table 10, a detailed analysis was conducted of the individual elections occurring in 1983. The other factors taken into consideration included characteristics of the election such as the number of workers eligible to vote, characteristics of the work force such as the percentage that was black, and characteristics of the union involved such as whether it was affiliated with the AFL-CIO or with the International Brotherhood of Teamsters.[17]

Adjustment of the union vote and success data to account for other influences does reduce somewhat the impact of hazard itself on election outcomes, but a strong positive association remains. When adjustment was made for other relevant factors, the presence of hazard gained unions an additional 9% of the votes cast, compared to the percentage of voters gained in safe industries. Given the closeness of the outcomes in many elections, this led to a union gain of 17% more of the elections in hazardous industries than of the elections in safe industries. The adjusted effects of injury rates themselves on election outcomes can be compared to the 24% higher union vote and 55% higher union success rate in hazardous as compared to safe industries using the unadjusted 1983 data in table 10.

Trends in Union Coverage of Hazardous Employments

The percentages of workers in hazardous and safe industries that were members of labor unions in 1971, 1977, and 1986, respectively, are displayed in table 11.[18] These figures were calculated using the Current Population Survey (CPS), a large household survey conducted every month by the U.S. Bureau of the Census. Industries are categorized as very hazardous, moderately hazardous, somewhat hazardous, or safe depending upon whether their rate of disabling occupational injuries and acute illnesses falls into the top, second, third, or fourth quartile of injury and illness rates for all industries. Consistent with the evidence on the desire of nonunion workers for union representation, hazardous jobs prove to be more heavily unionized than safe jobs. The general trend, however, is ominous for future attempts by workers to use collective bargaining to improve working conditions. The overall extent of union representation declined from 26% in 1971 to 25% in 1977 and then dropped dramatically to 18% in 1986. The sharp fall in the most recent decade was due to the closure of many unionized plants during the 1981–82 recession and to management's determination to open new plants on a strictly nonunion basis.

The greatest decline in union representation occurred in the most hazardous industries, where unionization was most extensive to begin with. After rising from 40% to 44% between 1971 and 1977, union representation fell to 28% in the most hazardous industries between 1977 and 1986. In contrast, representation in the safest industries rose from 12% to 20% between 1971 and 1977 and then fell to 14% in 1986, still slightly above the 1971 level.

Conclusion

The statistical evidence presented in this chapter lays to rest the paternalistic notion that American workers are unaware of most of the occupational safety and health hazards they face and are apathetic with regard to the hazards they do recognize. Almost one-third of female workers and more than

Table 11
*Percentage of Workers Belonging to Unions,
By Level of Hazard in Their Industries, 1971–1986*

	1971	*1977*	*1986*
All industries	25.6	24.8	17.6
Very hazardous industries	39.7	44.0	27.6
Moderately hazardous industries	36.9	30.6	17.2
Somewhat hazardous industries	20.3	14.8	9.2
Safest industries	11.7	19.6	14.2

one-third of male workers report facing at least one significant health or safety hazard on the job. Workers in occupations with considerable exposure to carcinogenic chemicals are substantially more likely to report exposure to dangerous chemicals and unhealthy conditions than are workers in occupations with less exposure to carcinogens. The statistical evidence suggests that workers faced with hazards on the job pursued voice strategies more frequently than they did exit strategies during the years under consideration. Unions initiate representation elections more frequently in industries with high injury rates than in industries with low injury rates. The ability of unions to gain new members has declined in recent years, however, and it is not clear how large a role unions will play in worker health and safety strategies in the future.

3

What Do Unions Do?

Workplace hazards are public health problems that often demand collective solutions. Chemical fumes, unguarded cutting blades, and infectious agents threaten all the workers exposed to them. As documented in the previous chapter, workers faced with health and safety risks frequently join labor unions as one way to deal with their problems. As worker and citizen concern for health and safety issues has grown over recent decades, unions have been presented with the opportunity to strengthen their activities in this area. What tactics have they developed to control occupational safety and health hazards? Once in place, what do labor unions do?

This chapter investigates recent trends in union involvement in occupational safety and health. Four related union activities are considered. First, unions improve the quantity and quality of information workers possess, both by ensuring worker access to medical and exposure records and by developing ways of generating new data. Second, unions protect workers who refuse to accept particularly hazardous assignments. Third, unions bargain collectively with management for improvements in working conditions and for the provision of protective equipment such as safety shoes and respirators. Finally, unions establish workplace health and safety committees that oversee hazard evaluations, worker training, protection of hazardous work refusals, and the direct control of workplace risks.

Labor unions embody the collective voice strategy in the private workplace. Unions believe strongly that workers should have a say in how health hazards are controlled and should not be limited to the "love it or leave" choice underlying the exit strategy. Recognizing the weak bargaining position of individual employees, unions emphasize collective endeavors. Government has supported collective bargaining to resolve workplace conflicts, thereby giving it an important public function. But compared with the judicial and regulatory mechanisms that will be discussed in later chapters, collective bargaining remains relatively private and independent of direct day-to-day interference by public bodies.

Labor Unions and the Worker's Access to Information on Workplace Hazards

Labor unions have a long history of seeking and winning access to information held by employers. The cornerstone of industrial relations policy in the United States, the National Labor Relations Act of 1935, requires that employers bargain in good faith over the terms of employment with the recognized representatives of their employees. As early as 1936, the National Labor Relations Board, which enforces the act, affirmed that the duty to bargain in good faith entailed a duty to provide the union with relevant information. The years since 1936 have been marked by the steady accumulation of precedent-setting cases in which the NLRB has extended the obligations of employers to provide information on wages, pension and health insurance plans, job classifications and job descriptions, overtime hours, layoffs, seniority lists, probation policies, equal opportunity programs, and other matters. The NLRB has taken a cautious attitude toward information purportedly involving trade secrets. In these situations, the board reasons that the union's need to know the information must be balanced against the firm's fear that the information might be disclosed to competitors.[1]

The issue of union access to information on workplace hazards and worker health came to a head in the late 1970s and early 1980s as a result of the efforts of two labor unions. The union interest in this matter was directly stimulated by the occupational sterilization case described in the Introduction. In 1977, the Oil, Chemical, and Atomic Workers International Union initiated a campaign to obtain disclosure of hazard information at many of the unionized chemical plants throughout the country. The national union provided local unions with a prototype letter to be sent to employers requesting information on hazard exposures and documented medical effects. One hundred ten of the local unions sent versions of this letter to employers. Over half of the employers responded positively to the union's requests and provided the information in some form, but several employers adopted an intransigent attitude and refused to supply any information at all. The OCAW focused its efforts on two recalcitrant firms, Minnesota Mining and Manufacturing and Colgate Palmolive. The union notified the NLRB that the two companies were violating their legal obligation to bargain in good faith. The union requested the chemical names of all substances used and produced in the plants, results of clinical and laboratory studies undertaken by the companies, lists of contaminants monitored by the companies, morbidity and mortality statistics on all past and present employees, plus other information related to radiation exposures, extremes of heat, noise levels, and Workers' Compensation claims. The International Chemical Workers Union (ICWU) adopted the OCAW strategy and encountered similar resistance. The ICWU filed a duty-to-bargain claim with the NLRB concerning the Borden Chemical company. Since the three cases raised similar issues, the NLRB reviewed them as a group.

The legal proceedings dragged on for several years. Finally, in April 1982, the board declared the three employers were violating their duty to bargain in good faith and required them to provide the unions with the requested information. "Few matters," the board said, "can be of greater legitimate concern to individuals in the workplace, and thus to the bargaining agent representing them, than exposure to conditions potentially threatening their health, well-being, or very lives."[2] The board did, however, make an exception for those chemicals considered trade secrets. While rejecting the employers' claims that their entire inventories of chemicals were trade secrets, the board accepted as legitimate their concerns for a small handful of chemicals whose very identity conveyed valuable information to competitors. The board instructed the two parties to bargain with each other as to the precise obligations employers have to provide sensitive information of this type.

In requiring direct disclosure to workers, the NLRB rejected two models of indirect disclosure that the employers had proposed. The employers argued that the Occupational Safety and Health Administration and other governmental bodies assured a safe and healthy workplace, thereby eliminating the need for worker self-help initiatives. The only information relevant to the union, the employers argued, would be the procedures developed to comply with governmental regulations. The NLRB rejected this argument by stressing the compatibility of collective bargaining with direct governmental regulation. The limitations of the regulatory approach in the absence of worker participation were well evidenced in the DBCP case that prompted the unions' interest in chemical hazard information.

The other model of indirect disclosure rejected by the NLRB concerned the potential role of the employer as a filter of hazard information to the worker. Borden Chemical had argued that raw data on chemical identities would be "irrelevant and misleading" to union members and that the company's own staff had already determined the toxic properties of the various chemicals. It proposed that worker information be limited to "a few simple handling and hygiene practices." This issue has turned out to be of paramount importance in the broader policy debate over the nature of the worker's right to know about workplace hazard exposures. Employers have often supported worker information policies as long as these were restricted to warnings and proper work practices, but have opposed policies that provided workers with detailed chemical and health data. This paternalistic approach denies the worker the ability to decide for himself or herself what is really hazardous and what must be done about it. It is based on an interpretation of occupational injuries and illnesses as caused by the failure of workers to follow rules set by management.

Gaining access to the employer's information on hazardous exposures and medical effects is only the first step in educating the workers as to the risks they face. Given the complexity of many of the hazards, and the detailed changes in work practices that are required to ensure safety, considerable training of individual workers is needed. Innovative labor unions are pushing for a greater role in the design and implementation of worker health and safety training programs. The United Automobile Workers (UAW), for example, has developed a particularly innovative set of programs for its members employed at General Motors and several other metalworking firms. In 1984 the UAW won an agreement from General Motors to create a special occupational safety and health training fund with payments of four cents for each hour worked by each union member. This fund would be controlled jointly by the company and the union and would be used to train union representatives, company supervisors, skilled-trades workers, and workers exposed to hazardous chemicals. In the program's first year, four new training courses were designed, covering asbestos, energy lockouts, manlift accidents, and lethal confined-space environments. These four hazards had been identified as major sources of on-the-job exposures and accidents in automobile factories.

The UAW has also negotiated similar training programs with other firms. UAW members employed at the Ford Motor Company benefit from a program conducted by the University of Michigan School of Public Health and the Michigan State

University Labor Education Program. At International Harvester, the union has a program in which union-appointed safety representatives conduct inspections and handle worker grievances while being paid their regular salaries.[3]

The diffusion of available hazard information through worker training programs presupposes that reliable information exists concerning the health effects of substances encountered on the job. But data of this sort are often lacking. Some hazards have escaped notice by employers and governmental agencies as well as by workers. In other instances employers have blocked efforts by researchers to study the health effects of toxic substances. With their control over access to the workplace, employers exert a very strong influence over which substances are studied and by whom. The potential abuses of this power have been documented most extensively in the case of asbestos, where the mining and milling interests concealed information on serious health effects for decades, which resulted in hundreds of thousands of asbestos-related diseases that might have been prevented.[4]

Most research in occupational epidemiology is conducted by scientists and physicians working in universities or government agencies. These researchers often produce studies of little immediate value to the workers at risk and have been notoriously reluctant to make their findings easily accessible to workers. Although some progress is being made by the National Institute for Occupational Safety and Health in informing workers whom research finds to be at high risk, there is generally only a very poor linkage between the concerns of workers and the priorities of researchers.[5]

Faced with the problem of unreliable or inaccessible data, some unions have themselves become involved in epidemiological research. In some instances they have sponsored research by university scientists or have collaborated with government researchers to ensure that the findings are made available to the work force. A few of the larger unions have developed the capacity to conduct their own studies, often combining the technical expertise of staff physicians and industrial hygienists with the enthusiasm of rank-and-file workers in a process called "barefoot epidemiology."

Union epidemiological efforts are necessarily modest in scope and must establish priorities very quickly. Unions frequently face reports of clusters of deaths or health problems among particular groups of workers and must determine whether these reports are valid. Anecdotal evidence must be evaluated to determine whether the problem warrants a full-fledged epidemiological study, a more modest program of continued monitoring, or an effort to reassure workers that occupational factors are not a cause. The United Automobile Workers has developed an epidemiological "triage" program of this sort.[6]

In the early 1980s, the local UAW union representing workers at a metal-stamping plant in Kalamazoo, Michigan, became concerned about reports of a possibly high rate of cancer among its members. It began collecting death statistics and called in the help of the national union's health and safety staff. The UAW staff conducted an industrial hygiene tour of the facility and identified an area of concern. The floors in the plant consisted of wood blocks that were set and protected with hot coal tar in an operation that closely resembled roof tarring. Several epidemiological studies had previously found that roofers exposed to hot coal tar were at increased risk of cancer. Millwrights responsible for laying the floor tar were exposed to smoke and vapors in their work. They also worked closely with maintenance welders who flame cut floor bolts; sometimes the tar and the wood blocks ignited. The wood blocks had been treated with wood preservatives and had also absorbed solvent and oil spills.

The union decided to conduct an epidemiological study, which necessitated an extensive search through death records. They discovered that the number of cancer deaths among workers was twice that of people of similar age and sex in the general population. Excess risks were identified for leukemia and cancers of the digestive organs and lungs. The union brought the results of its study to the attention of the employer. After some discussion, the employer agreed to take steps to reduce exposures. The firm purchased new electric tar pots and agreed to obtain portable ventilation units, construct several welding booths with special exhaust systems, purchase additional respirators, and search for floor coating substitutes. A series of educational meetings was held with more than 200 affected workers in the plant. At the urging of the union, the employer sent a bulletin to its other plants asking that floor tarring operations be evaluated and that steps be taken to reduce emissions and search for substitute materials. Air sampling conducted after the installation of the new tar pots showed large reductions in hazardous emissions.

The Right to Refuse Hazardous Work

Historically, worker refusals to perform especially hazardous assignments were simply another manifestation of labor's most commonly used approach to resolving problems, the strike. Union organizations strengthened hazardous work refusals by increasing the number of participants. The National Labor Relations Act of 1935 supported hazardous work refusals by requiring employers to bargain in good faith and by designating work refusals as concerted actions that are specifically protected under the act.[7] Employers may not discharge workers participating in concerted actions. This protection of hazardous work refusals is significant in that no objective proof of hazard is required. If the workers believe in good faith that conditions are hazardous, then their action falls under the provisions of the act. However, the workers' right to protection under the National Labor Relations Act can be bargained away by unions that agree to a no-strike clause in the union-management contract. Management has successfully inserted such no-strike clauses in many contracts in order to prevent shop floor discontent from interrupting the production process.

Union-management relationships in the United States center around contracts that cover wages and other terms of employment for a fixed period of time. These contracts are renegotiated periodically, and strikes are most common at negotiation times. During the period when a signed contract is in force, disputes between the union and management are usually resolved through the grievance and arbitration mechanism rather than through strikes. This tends to be the case whether or not an explicit no-strike clause has been included in the contract. The typical union-management grievance mechanism is structured in the form of a hierarchy of reviews. Grievances that cannot be resolved at low levels move up through the system. The upper levels of the grievance system involve the higher levels of management and the union. The final step in the process usually imposes binding arbitration by an impartial outsider.

Hazardous work refusals can enter the union grievance mechanism in the same fashion as other discipline cases. Since the grievance mechanism is designed primarily as a way to interpret the written contract, some unions find it advantageous to bargain explicitly for the right of workers to refuse imminently hazardous tasks. In 1980, approximately one-fourth of union contracts had hazardous work refusal clauses.[8] These contract clauses can protect hazardous work refusals even in the absence of objective proof of hazard and in the presence of a no-strike clause.

The union grievance mechanism has certain limitations. As mentioned earlier, the ultimate step in the grievance system usually is binding arbitration. The interpretation of hazardous work refusals is therefore subject to the beliefs and values of the arbitrators. The arbitration system is a form of private U.S. labor law that has its own traditions and principles. It evolved out of the militant shop floor struggles of the 1930s and 1940s, when direct action was the primary response to dissatisfaction with working conditions and other terms of employment. The arbitration system embodies the view that direct action of this sort is unacceptable. The appropriate response is for dissatisfied workers to continue working but file a grievance. This perspective has been formalized into the "work now, grieve later" principle.

Most arbitrators focus on upholding management authority while compensating individual workers who have meritorious complaints. This has tended to shift the burden onto the worker of proving there is a legitimate hazard. Of the published arbitration decisions analyzed in one study, 154 concerned hazardous work refusals and 120 of these had an identifiable standard of proof.[9] Fully two-thirds of the decisions required objective evidence that the working conditions were hazardous, as opposed to accepting evidence that the workers believed in good faith that the conditions were hazardous. Examples of objective proof included measured airborne concentrations of asbestos, the results of federal or state agency inspections, Geiger counter readings of radiation levels, photographs, and the personal observations of the arbitrators themselves. Acceptable worker testimony as to the seriousness of the hazards covered welding operations being performed outdoors in thunderstorms, unannounced blasting that shook an underground lunchroom where miners were eating and caused lunch and helmets to tumble on the floor, and a malfunctioning punch press that required workers to place their hands within a point of operation that was still stained with blood from a previous serious accident. In one-third of the arbitration rulings, a good faith standard of proof was used. Here the work refusal was considered legitimate if the worker or workers truly believed the conditions posed an imminent hazard, regardless of whether there existed objective proof.

Recognizing the limitations on union grievance and arbitration systems, in 1973 OSHA promulgated a standard to protect workers who refuse to work because of hazardous conditions. Workers walking off the job in response to health and safety hazards are protected from reprisals if the work refusal satisfies three criteria. First, the worker must have a "reasonable" fear that the working conditions present a danger of death or serious injury. Second, there must be insufficient time to utilize the normal remedies existing under the 1970

Occupational Safety and Health Act, which consist of work-place inspection and court-ordered injunction. Third, the worker must have made an attempt to remedy the hazard through consultation with the employer. This standard provides an alternative source of support for workers covered by union grievance and arbitration mechanisms and also extends to nonunion workers. It was quickly contested by management.

An incident at the Whirlpool Corporation during the 1970s led to a test of the legality of the 1973 OSHA standard. Whirlpool manufactured household appliances at a plant in Ohio, in which thirteen miles of overhead conveyors moved parts from one area to another. Screens had been installed underneath these conveyors to catch the parts that occasionally slipped off. Workers were required to walk out onto these screens to retrieve fallen parts or to repair the screens themselves. The screens were dilapidated in some parts of the factory, and sometimes workers broke through them. The workers complained to management about the risks posed by the unsafe screens, and management began to replace the older sections. Before this replacement work was completed, however, a maintenance worker fell through an old part of the screen and was killed. After this incident, two other maintenance workers were instructed to perform work on similarly dilapidated sections of the screen, even after they had repeatedly complained to management about the conditions. When the two workers refused the work order, they were suspended through the end of the shift and letters of reprimand were placed in their permanent personnel files. The case was brought to the attention of OSHA, which sought a reversal of the disciplinary actions under the terms of the 1973 hazardous work refusal standard. The case was eventually appealed up to the Supreme Court, which unanimously upheld the OSHA standard and ruled in favor of the two workers.

While the Supreme Court's ruling in the Whirlpool case might appear to protect workers refusing work in the face of imminent dangers, it actually leaves a considerable residue of uncertainty. The OSHA work refusal standard applies only to situations where the worker's fear of death or bodily harm is "reasonable." At the time he or she is contemplating a work refusal, therefore, the worker cannot be sure of being protected by the OSHA standard. This poses severe problems when the worker's concern is for subtle risks such as cancer that may occur years in the future. Here the worker is at the mercy of a reinterpretation of the scientific evidence that shows his or her fears were unfounded.

In summary, unions have strengthened the ability of workers to refuse hazardous assignments without being penalized, but the protection is very incomplete. The grievance and arbitration mechanism is the most widely used method for reviewing hazardous work refusals; in many cases it produces satisfactory outcomes. It relies ultimately on the values and traditions of professional arbitrators, however, who often view hazardous work refusals as a direct affront to their "work now, grieve later" principle. The OSHA hazardous work refusal standard is potentially far-reaching but is limited by its reliance upon an objective standard for proving hazard. Realistically, the OSHA standard is of most use to workers who have a labor union supporting them in the often lengthy process of filing a complaint with the agency.

Collective Bargaining for Job Safety and Health

With the exception of some organizations that represent workers in especially hazardous industries, U.S. labor unions were slow to adopt health and safety conditions as a major topic of collective bargaining.[10] Historically, companies claimed that occupational safety and health were entirely within management's prerogative, but in 1966 the NLRB ruled that safety was a mandatory bargaining issue. Firms were henceforth obligated to discuss safety and health with the union, although they were not obligated to accede to any of the union's demands.

While it is difficult to measure the extent of collective bargaining concerning job safety and health issues, two complementary data sources shed some light. The Bureau of National Affairs (BNA), a private, Washington-based organization, has maintained a file of collectively bargained contracts and monitored the topics they cover since the 1950s. The file contains over 5,000 contracts and is kept up-to-date with new contract changes. Contracts are deleted from the file when the bargaining relationship is terminated, as in the case of a plant closure. A sample of approximately 400 contracts, chosen to represent a wide variety of industries and unions, is analyzed periodically.[11] The second data source is a series of analyses performed by the U.S. Bureau of Labor Statistics between 1970 and 1980 of all union contracts covering 1,000 or more workers, supplemented by occasional earlier studies.[12] This series of reports was terminated in 1981 due to cutbacks in bureau funding.

There has been clear growth in collective bargaining concerning health and safety since the 1950s. As the data in table 12 indicate, 69% of BNA manufacturing contracts and 38% of BNA nonmanufacturing contracts made some mention of safety in 1957, but 89% of the manufacturing contracts and 77% of the nonmanufacturing contracts made some mention in 1987. The upward trend in union activity is clear, with the major increase occurring after the passage of the Occupational Safety and Health Act in 1970. This acceleration highlights the influence of governmental regulatory activities on private workplace initiatives to improve safety and health.

The degree of confidence that may be placed in the BNA data is enhanced by a comparison with several isolated studies conducted during the 1950s. A national survey of 2,411 contracts performed in 1950 by the U.S. Bureau of Labor Statistics found that 56% of manufacturing contracts and 40% of nonmanufacturing contracts contained safety provisions.[13] In 1951, the California Department of Industrial Relations surveyed 1,928 contracts in that state, of which 47% were found to contain safety clauses of one type or another.[14]

Table 12
Percentage of Union Contracts Covering
Selected Issues in Workplace Health and Safety
(Bureau of National Affairs Sample)

	1957	1961	1966	1971	1979	1983	1987
Any safety clause							
Manufacturing	69	71	69	71	87	87	89
Nonmanufacturing	38	48	48	52	73	72	77
General duty clause							
Manufacturing	43	39	43	48	58	64	66
Nonmanufacturing	12	20	19	28	36	38	43
Joint safety committee							
Manufacturing	31	34	35	38	55	57	62
Nonmanufacturing	12	14	18	19	24	26	27
Ongoing physical exams	12	14	10	17	22	23	22

The most common type of health and safety clause in collectively bargained contracts is the general statement of management's responsibility for providing a safe work environment. In the BNA data, general duty clauses were found in 66% of manufacturing contracts and 43% of nonmanufacturing contracts in 1987, up from 43% and 12%, respectively, in 1957. The general duty clause may refer to cooperation with the union or consistency with public laws and standards. Some of these statements are just empty acknowledgments of the issue and carry no real content. In other instances, however, they play a very significant role by bringing safety-related issues under the purview of the contract and thus of the grievance and arbitration system. Workers and their union representatives have the right to raise safety and health issues through these latter channels, where some amount of equity is ensured, rather than being open to summary rejection by lower-level management personnel.

While a general duty clause guarantees workers and unions the right to use the grievance and arbitration system, it does not ensure a favorable outcome from that process. Some contracts include clauses specifying particular safeguards. These clauses cover environmental conditions such as lighting, temperature, noise, radiation, fire hazards, and exposure to noxious gases and dusts. For example, the 1974 agreement between U.S. Steel and the United Steelworkers Union of America specified precise engineering controls that were to be installed to limit carcinogenic emissions from coke ovens at the Clairton, Pennsylvania, mill.[15] According to the BLS data presented in table 13, 16% of manufacturing contracts and 6% of nonmanufacturing contracts mandated some kind of environmental protections in 1980. A 1983 analysis of 963 responses to a survey of firms belonging to the National Federation of Independent Business found that unionized firms were significantly more likely than nonunion firms to undertake any of twelve specified activities to abate hazards. Among the unionized firms, approximately one-fourth reported that safety issues were important elements in the collective bargaining process.[16]

Collective bargaining to achieve union access to employers' records on hazard exposures and medical effects was evidenced in a 1974–75 survey of contracts conducted by the U.S. Bureau of Labor Statistics. Sixteen percent of the contracts analyzed in that study required management to provide the union with any safety-related information it possessed.[17] These contract clauses guaranteed such things as information on the toxic materials being used, the results of workplace monitoring performed by the company, reports of lost-time accidents, and copies of Workers' Compensation data.[18] Some contracts required management to monitor exposure levels or provide monitoring equipment to the union-management health and safety committee.

Some unions have bargained for hazard pay premiums. During the 1970s, hazard pay clauses were found in approximately 10% of large manufacturing contracts and in 30% of large nonmanufacturing contracts, mostly in the construction and transportation industries. The prevalence of hazard pay

Table 13
Percentage of Union Contracts Covering Selected Issues in Workplace Health and Safety
(Bureau of Labor Statistics Sample)

	1970	1971	1972	1973	1974	1975	1976	1978	1980
Environmental protections									
Manufacturing	—	11.7	12.6	10.0	11.5	14.0	14.0	15.1	16.4
Nonmanufacturing	—	7.9	4.6	4.7	5.7	6.7	6.0	5.9	6.3
Safety equipment									
Manufacturing	47.6	52.3	51.7	51.8	52.8	56.3	56.5	58.0	58.7
Nonmanufacturing	35.0	35.3	42.9	43.8	47.0	48.0	46.1	51.0	49.5
Joint safety committee									
Manufacturing	39.6	39.2	36.5	39.0	38.2	40.6	44.7	47.6	55.0
Nonmanufacturing	16.7	18.2	15.8	15.3	16.6	16.7	16.3	18.1	19.9
Right to refuse hazardous work									
Manufacturing	—	—	—	—	14.8	16.7	16.6	17.3	26.3
Nonmanufacturing	—	—	—	—	25.0	26.1	24.7	26.5	24.9
Hazard pay									
Manufacturing	—	9.4	10.7	11.6	11.0	9.6	10.2	10.0	9.8
Nonmanufacturing	—	30.3	29.4	28.8	28.7	31.0	29.8	29.8	31.2

provisions did not change over the course of the 1970s, as the data in table 13 attest. Other contract clauses focus on the financial impacts of job-related injuries and illnesses. Of particular importance are rate retention, job transfer, and seniority rights for workers unable to do their former jobs but able to do some other kind of work. Some contracts guarantee retention of benefits and accrual of seniority for workers unable to do any work for a certain period of time due to job-related injury or illness.[19]

An important category of contract clauses guarantees the rights of workers and their union representatives in the pursuit of safety and health objectives. The employer may be required to pay workers for time spent accompanying OSHA inspectors or while engaged in other safety activities. Although the 1970 Occupational Safety and Health Act prohibits retaliation against workers for calling in an OSHA inspector, some unions find it wise to include such guarantees in their contracts in order to permit enforcement through the grievance and arbitration system.

Joint Union-Management Committees

An effective mechanism for union participation in day-to-day health and safety matters is the joint union-management health and safety committee. In principle, these committees meet regularly to discuss problems and propose remedies. They give the union a continuous platform from which to deliver its demands, and provide the firm with a means for canvassing the opinions of its employees, as filtered by the union. Joint committees may be established by a contract clause but need not be.

Contract clauses mandating joint union-management safety and health committees have become fairly common, doubling from 31% to 62% in manufacturing and from 12% to 27% in nonmanufacturing between 1957 and 1987. Safety committees were mandated in 14% of the contracts surveyed by the BLS in 1954 and 1955.[20] In the BLS sample of contracts covering more than 1,000 workers, safety committee provisions grew over the course of the 1970s from 40% to 55% in manufacturing and from 17% to 20% in nonmanufacturing. The influence of OSHA on management's willingness to establish joint committees was shown in a 1975 survey of approximately fifty firms in New York State whose employees were represented by the International Association of Machinists. Half of the forty-two existing committees had been established in the four years since the passage of the Occupational Safety and Health Act.[21]

Union-management health and safety committees are generally oriented toward day-to-day fluctuations in working conditions rather than toward the major technological determinants of injuries and illnesses. Both management and union respondents to the survey conducted in New York State felt that while OSHA had a major impact on the adoption of safer technologies, the joint committees did not. The committees were seen as concerned with general housekeeping, temperature, dust, and fire protection. This union emphasis on hazard identification rather than hazard reduction was also reported in a 1984 survey.[22] Fully 70% of the survey respondents rated their health and safety committees as effective in identifying hazards, while only 42% considered the committees effective in reducing injuries and illnesses. While half of the committees surveyed had the nominal authority to implement recommendations on their own, only one-fourth had a budget to do so. However, a study of union-management committees in the construction industry credited cooperative programs with a 40% reduction in injuries and a 20% increase in productivity.[23]

The growth in union-management committees is particularly striking when compared with the small fraction of contracts that directly mandate improvements in working conditions. This disparity reveals quite a bit about the current status and future prospects for labor union health and safety efforts. With some exceptions, labor unions do not possess exceptional expertise on the health effects of and the technological alternatives to toxic substances. The conditions faced by workers often vary from workplace to workplace and sometimes from month to month. It is difficult for the union leadership to invest a substantial proportion of its resources and bargaining power in the direct control of particular hazards. From the union's point of view, therefore, it is preferable to treat occupational health and safety as an area of cooperation rather than of conflict with management. The collective bargaining process focuses on topics that are inherently conflictual, such as wages, fringe benefits, and job security. The union focus on joint committees for health and safety embodies an attempt to partially insulate that issue from the collective bargaining process.

Conclusion

American labor unions are becoming increasingly involved in all aspects of occupational safety and health. They are striving to raise membership awareness of health and safety risks, pressuring management to divulge exposure and medical data, designing and implementing worker training programs, and conducting new epidemiological studies. Unions also help workers reduce the level of risk. The individual worker's ability to refuse exceptionally hazardous assignments is strengthened by the union's grievance and arbitration mechanism, which ensures procedural justice in shop floor disputes. Unions can address the underlying causes of occupational injuries and illnesses by bargaining for direct improvements in working conditions and by establishing joint union-management health and safety committees to monitor conditions. However, the past three decades have witnessed a major offensive by employers against unions and collective bargaining. Unions have successfully withstood the employer offensive in some industries, but there has been a steep decline in the fraction of private sector workers represented by unions. This decline in private sector unionism is having an enormous impact on the ability of workers to cope with the health and safety hazards they face on the job.

Thus the role played by labor unions in occupational safety and health is characterized by both cooperation and conflict. In strongly unionized workplaces, both management and labor are coming to view health and safety as an area of potential cooperation, partially distinct from the conflictual collective bargaining process. This common perspective is symbolized by the growth of joint health and safety committees, which outnumber other cooperative efforts.[24] However, management adopts this cooperative stance only where union organization seems inevitable. Elsewhere, health and safety remains an area of conflict, with the balance of power resting decisively on management's side.

4

Worker Productivity and Corporate Profits

Workers pursue a variety of individual and collective strategies in response to health and safety hazards. At one extreme, they quit and leave the dangers behind them. At the other, they join labor unions and bargain with their employers to improve working conditions. In between, they adopt an often inchoate mix of strategies: partially conflictual and partially cooperative, sometimes spontaneous and sometimes premeditated. Absenteeism, cajolery, vandalism, safety committees, OSHA complaints, Workers' Compensation claims, media publicity, "wrongful discharge" lawsuits—each offers new possibilities.

But this is not the whole picture. Management has the responsibility to earn the highest possible rate of profit and has traditionally resisted any infringement on its authority to organize and supervise the process of production. Shop floor worker initiatives to improve working conditions often threaten unilateral management authority and hence generate counterinitiatives to protect that authority. Performance reviews, transfers, demotions, discharges, job redesign, subcontracting, plant closures—each offers a means for reasserting managerial control.

Occupational safety and health hazards produce moves and countermoves by employees and employers, each pursuing their own objectives. In part these objectives are congruent: both labor and management benefit from high productivity that permits generous wages and enviable profits. In part the objectives conflict: labor and management invariably disagree as to the appropriate distribution of revenue between wages and profits. The mutual benefits potentially available from cooperation soften the edges of disagreement. Conversely, industrial conflict over wages and profits undermines cooperation, impairs productivity, and reduces future wages and profits. The industrial relations system is a mix of formal and informal laws, accepted procedures, and rules of thumb that seek to adjudicate conflicting claims and reduce adverse effects on matters of mutual benefit. Worker responses to occupational safety and health hazards can be understood properly only within the larger industrial relations context.

In highlighting the impact of worker voice strategies on industrial relations and economic performance, this chapter develops a broader perspective than that adopted previously. The emphasis now is on how the efforts by workers to improve conditions and the efforts by management to reassert authority impose burdens upon society as a whole. Workplace hazards produce injuries and illnesses, the costs of which are borne in large part by public health care and disability programs. Equally important are the social costs of lost production due to labor-management conflict. The public has a large stake in the process and outcome of industrial relations in the private sector.

Industrial Relations and Economic Productivity

Workers can impede production in many ways. Their tactics are often hard to detect and, even when detected, hard to combat. Absenteeism and "Monday morning sickness" are often associated with employee dissatisfaction. Through slowdowns and "working to rule," workers can pressure management simply by refusing to provide the extra effort and ingenuity habitually offered in order to get the job done well. A more visible expression of dissatisfaction is the strike, which may be an orderly event occurring at the end of a scheduled contract period or a sudden "wildcat" event occurring around a new issue.

Needless to say, worker pressure tactics are unlikely to go unpunished by management. Individual workers or small groups may be disciplined with suspensions or demotions, and particularly militant workers may be fired. The efficacy of these short-term management responses is limited, since they may generate even more worker dissatisfaction. Longer-term management strategies may reduce the cost of worker dissatisfaction and turnover by reducing the level of on-the-job training in hazardous jobs. Job tasks are then governed rigidly by rules, rather than being left to worker discretion. Alternatively, management may structure the employment relationship so as to encourage worker cooperation and reduce dissatisfaction. Wage increases always help in this regard but may prove to be a costly means to the desired end. More direct responses to worker dissatisfaction include formalized mechanisms for dispute resolution and team approaches to decision making that permit a limited amount of worker participation.

Productivity depends on the effort expended by workers and management separately and their ability to cooperate and work effectively together. Dissatisfied and uncooperative workers still must be paid, even if they are not producing much. Management can fire them but then must hire and train replacements. This requires management time that could instead be directly spent in improving productivity. And, of course, the new workers may eventually adopt the attitudes and behavior patterns of those they replaced.

When hazard-related industrial conflict reduces employee productivity, it raises employer costs. Each worker produces less output than he or she would in a better work environment, and therefore each unit of output that is produced requires more worker hours. Each of these hours must be paid. Similar increases in costs occur if poor industrial relations lead to an underutilization of machinery or a waste of materials. Hazard-related conflict therefore impacts corporate profits, which are simply the difference between total revenues and total costs. If costs increase, firms will try to defend their profit rates by raising prices. Competition from other firms places sharp limits, however, on management's ability to defend profits in this way.

Indexes of Worker Morale: Dissatisfaction and Absenteeism

Worker dissatisfaction is a good starting point for a study of industrial conflict in hazardous jobs. If workers could quit bad jobs and easily find better ones, then we would not observe persistent dissatisfaction. Alternatively, if employers could design personnel policies that effectively responded to employee concerns, then dissatisfaction would dissipate quickly. If levels of dissatisfaction are higher in hazardous jobs than in safe ones, this indicates that neither the exit strategy nor cooperative labor-management programs have been successful in coping with worker concerns about unsafe and unhealthy working conditions.

The 1977 Quality of Employment Survey, the 1978 and 1980 National Longitudinal Surveys, and the 1984 AFL-CIO survey, described in chapter 2, queried workers concerning satisfaction with their jobs. The measure of job dissatisfaction discussed here is provided by workers who report being strongly dissatisfied; mildly dissatisfied workers are treated as if they are satisfied.[1] Dissatisfaction can be most easily conceptualized as a discordance between the quality of the job the worker has and the quality of the job the worker feels he or she deserves. To the extent that workers in hazardous jobs have low expectations, one would not expect them to express dissatisfaction more frequently than workers in safe jobs. In order to account for the factors influencing worker expectations, therefore, one must statistically adjust for differences in workers' education, job tenure, age, and race. In order to identify the special influence of health and safety hazards, it is also important to account for characteristics of the jobs, such as wages, training possibilities, promotion possibilities, and employment security.

Workers who perceive their jobs as hazardous are substantially more likely than workers who perceive their jobs as safe to be strongly dissatisfied, as the data collected in table 14 indicate. The QES, which represents workers of all ages, shows that the presence of hazard raises the probability that a male worker will report dissatisfaction by 80% and more than triples the probability that a female worker will report dissatisfaction. The association is weaker in the NLS, which focused on young workers. Exposure to hazardous conditions raises the probability that an NLS woman will report job dissatisfaction by 40%. Slightly more NLS men in safe jobs report dissatisfaction than NLS men in hazardous jobs, after adjusting for other job and worker characteristics. This is due to the fact that NLS men in hazardous jobs report so many other undesirable job characteristics in addition to hazard, characteristics that are themselves very strongly associated with dissatisfaction. When one examines the level of dissatisfaction in

Table 14

Adjusted Percentage of Workers in Hazardous and Safe Jobs
Reporting Job Dissatisfaction

	Men			Women		
	Hazardous Jobs	Safe Jobs	Ratio	Hazardous Jobs	Safe Jobs	Ratio
1977 QES	16.4	9.1	1.80	23.8	7.3	3.26
1978–80 NLS	7.1	7.8	0.91	9.6	6.8	1.41
1984 AFL	13.8	11.6	1.19	11.5	6.5	1.77

hazardous and safe jobs, not adjusting for other job characteristics, one finds rates of dissatisfaction among NLS men in hazardous jobs to be 40% higher than rates in safe jobs.[2] Among the AFL survey respondents, exposure to workplace hazards raised the adjusted fraction of men reporting dissatisfaction by 19% and the adjusted fraction of women reporting dissatisfaction by almost 80%.

Chronic absenteeism is a sure mark of worker indifference to management's goals. In some cases it may be an intentional form of pressure, as in the case of organized "sick-outs" in response to some grievance. For example, "Monday morning sickness" is frequently a symptom of an ailing industrial relations system. Two published studies of absenteeism have examined the influence of workplace hazards. The first considered monthly production and absenteeism data for 1976 from forty-one plants in the paper industry.[3] Absenteeism was measured as the ratio of absent days to total days scheduled. Days lost due to occupational injuries themselves were first subtracted out, thereby allowing the analysis to focus on work absences not directly related to disability. These data were adjusted for wages and fringe benefits, employment levels, the rate of hiring, and other relevant factors. The second study used data from the 1973 Quality of Employment Survey, a precursor of the 1977 QES, which included workers from all industries.[4] The 1973 survey recorded the number of days each respondent missed from work during the prior two weeks. The effect of workplace injury rates was statistically adjusted for the effects of wages and fringe benefits, worker demographic characteristics, and other factors. Unsafe working conditions proved to be the single most important and consistent determinant of absenteeism in both studies. In the paper industry, a 10 percent increase in the injury rate caused the absenteeism rate to increase by one-third. Workers in the 1973 survey who were exposed to hazardous conditions were absent from work twice as often as comparable workers not exposed to hazards.

Indexes of Industrial Conflict:
Discharges and Strikes

It is very difficult to measure management responses to worker health and safety strategies. Many different carrot-and-stick approaches are conceivable. Wage increases are one prominent carrot; the stick of discipline may be used at least as often. Discipline can occur along a gradient of increasing severity, from reprimand through demotion to discharge. It would be desirable to measure whether each type of discipline is used in responding to worker health and safety initiatives. The available data restrict us, however, to management responses at the high end of the severity scale.

Rates of discharges (firings) in hazardous and safe manufacturing industries surveyed by the U.S. Bureau of Labor Statistics in 1977 are documented in the first row of table 15. These figures have been adjusted for differences among industries in other factors likely to influence industrial relations, in a manner analogous to that used with the worker survey data on dissatisfaction.[5] The adjusted discharge rates reveal the influence of hazardous working conditions on worker militancy and management disciplinary responses. More than 5% of the workers employed in industries with injury rates above the

Table 15
*Adjusted Rates of Discharges and Strikes per 100 Workers
in Hazardous and Safe Industries*

	Hazardous Industries	Safe Industries	Ratio
Annual discharge rate			
1977 BLS (manufacturing)	5.4	3.1	1.74
Annual strike rate			
1976–78 BLS (manufacturing)	4.5	2.9	1.55
1976–78 PSID (all sectors)	9.2	5.5	1.67
1985–87 PSID (all sectors)	3.2	2.3	1.39

average were fired in 1977, 75% more than in industries with below-average injury rates.

Worker dissatisfaction with hazardous working conditions can result in individual acts of insubordination or militancy, such as refusals to work without additional training. These individual grievances can coalesce into collective actions, most visibly in a strike. Strikes are good measures of poor industrial relations because they are economically irrational. During a strike, workers lose wages and the company loses profits. Both sides are worse off than they would be if somehow they could have resolved their differences without a strike. The fact that they cannot find a mutually acceptable solution without a show of strength indicates a low level of trust and cooperation.

In analyzing strikes, it is desirable to combine several years of data because union contracts in the United States are often negotiated only every three years. The best source of information on strikes is the comprehensive data on manufacturing industries maintained by the U.S. Bureau of Labor Statistics until 1981; the 1976–78 figures are used here. The second source of strike data is the Panel Study of Income Dynamics, the longitudinal worker survey used in chapter 2.[6] The PSID asked workers whether they had spent any time on strike during the past twelve months. In order to ensure comparability with the BLS manufacturing data, the PSID surveys covering 1976–78 are considered here. The 1985–87 PSID data also are analyzed, so as to obtain insights into hazard-related industrial conflict during the 1980s. The PSID data provide a useful complement to the BLS figures because they cover nonmanufacturing, as well as manufacturing, workers. Both the BLS and PSID strike data are adjusted for job and worker characteristics aside from health and safety hazards that might be expected to influence strike rates.[7]

During the 1970s, strike rates in manufacturing were 50% higher in industries with injury rates above the manufacturing average than in comparable manufacturing industries with below-average injury rates, as statistics in the second row of table 15 indicate. The same general pattern is found among PSID respondents. Employment in an industry with above-average injury rates raised by two-thirds the probability that a PSID worker participated in a strike over the course of the year, as data in the third row of the table testify. These hazard-related differences in strike rates are comparable to the differences reported in other studies covering the same period.[8]

The 1980s witnessed a dramatic drop in strike rates compared with the previous decade. With the rapid growth of nonunion competition, unionized firms adopted a much harder line in collective bargaining. Unions, in turn, sought other tactics. From the 1970s to the 1980s the percentage of unionized PSID workers involved in strikes declined by 65% in hazardous industries and by 58% in safe industries. Although strikes continued to occur more frequently in hazardous than in safe industries, the differential declined to 39%, as evidenced by the data in the fourth row of table 15.

The strike data presented in table 15 include both authorized strikes occurring at the time union contracts are renegotiated and wildcat strikes occurring during the course of the contract. Authorized strikes are far more common. Wildcat strike data are important in their own right, however, since these spontaneous events are often direct expressions of worker discontent. One published study examined the determinants of wildcat strikes in manufacturing industries over the period between 1960 and 1977. After adjusting other industry characteristics, manufacturing industries experiencing high and increasing injury rates had substantially higher rates of wildcat strikes than did industries with low and stable injury rates.[9]

Productivity in Manufacturing Industries

The strong association between workplace hazards, dissatisfaction, absenteeism, discharges, and strikes suggests that hazard-related industrial conflict dampens productivity. A number of economic studies have examined the effect of industrial relations on the performance of the economy. In every study, poor industrial relations are found to be associated with low productivity. The rate of growth in manufacturing output per production worker was adversely affected by wildcat strikes over the 1961 to 1981 period.[10] Productivity was lower and production costs were higher in the automobile industry in years with high rates of grievances, quits, and wildcat strikes.[11] Productivity and product quality in General Motors automobile plants were adversely affected by grievances, absenteeism, and worker discipline actions between 1970 and 1979.[12] A case study of productivity in the paper industry found output levels to be significantly higher in the months with fewer injuries.[13] This latter study is particularly interesting since it focuses on injury rates and is based on detailed information at the plant level; thus there is no possibility that the differences in productivity could have been caused by plant-specific differences in technology, management expertise, or worker skill and training.

The most comprehensive data on productivity are collected by the U.S. Department of Commerce as part of its annual survey of manufacturing establishments. Each year the department queries a representative sample of firms in each of 450 manufacturing industries concerning inputs consumed and outputs produced. The input and output data for each manufacturing industry have been linked across years from 1959 to 1978.[14] Insights into the influence of hazardous working conditions on productivity can be obtained by comparing these input and output data with rates of disabling injuries and illnesses, also published on an annual basis.[15] To simplify the discussion, productivity levels are presented here for five evenly spaced years that span the 1959 to 1978 period, rather than for all twenty individual years.

Rates of output per production worker hour in hazardous and safe manufacturing industries over a twenty-year period,

Table 16
*Adjusted Value of Output per Production Worker Hour
in Hazardous and Safe Manufacturing Industries
(in 1972 Dollars)*

	Hazardous Industries	Safe Industries	Ratio
1959	16.34	16.42	0.99
1963	18.08	18.80	0.96
1968	21.12	21.80	0.97
1973	24.29	25.86	0.94
1978	25.94	29.60	0.88

adjusted for energy, capital, raw material, and nonproduction labor inputs, are presented in table 16. Productivity was lower in hazardous industries than in safe industries in every year. The magnitude of the hazard-related difference in productivity grew during this period. In 1959, labor productivity in hazardous industries was 1% less than labor productivity in safe industries.[16] By 1978, productivity in hazardous industries was 12% less than in safe industries. This divergence resulted from substantially lower rates of productivity growth in hazardous as compared with safe industries, particularly in the first and last five years of the period. From 1959 to 1963, for example, productivity increased by 14.5% in safe industries but by only 10.6% in hazardous industries. The difference is even more striking for the 1973 to 1978 period, during which productivity in safe industries again grew by 14.5% while productivity in hazardous industries grew by only 6.8%. It is not clear why growth rates should diverge during these particular periods. One characteristic of these periods, however, was the poor overall state of the U.S. economy. Both the end of the 1950s and the middle of the 1970s were marked by sharp recessions in consumer and investment spending and a corresponding surge in unemployment. The rate of unemployment for manufacturing workers averaged 6.3% in 1959–63,

3.8% in 1964–68, 5.1% in 1969–73, and 7.4% in 1974–78. It may be that workplace hazards have the greatest adverse effect on productivity during periods of general economic stress, when labor-management relations can quickly shift from cooperation to conflict.

Workplace Hazards and Corporate Profits

If management could compensate for lower productivity and higher production costs by raising the prices it charges to consumers, then no difference would be observed between profit rates in hazardous and safe industries. There is no reason to assume, however, that such price increases are possible. Competition from producers with safer technologies will prevent firms from fully passing on the cost of hazard-related industrial conflict. In general, prices will be based on what the market will bear, which has no strong relationship to industrial relations and productivity on the shop floor.

The ideal measure of corporate profits would reflect long-term expected differences as well as short-term actual differences between revenues and costs, but the paucity of data forces us to focus on short-term profits. Two measures are readily available. The "price-cost margin," obtained from 1977 Department of Commerce data, is calculated as the value of industry output minus the costs of materials and payroll, divided by value of output. This measure can be conceptualized as the short-term annual difference between revenues and costs (net revenue), measured as a fraction of total revenue. The "return on capital" measure of profitability is the ratio of net revenue to capital assets, as reported to the Internal Revenue Service for 1979–81. This differs conceptually from the price-cost margin in expressing the profit rate as a ratio of net revenue to the value of assets rather than to the value of total revenue.[17]

When studying the association between workplace hazards and corporate profits, it is necessary to take into account other influences on profits. Most important among these are the degree of concentration in the industry, the ease of entry into the industry by new firms, the extent of union power, and changes in consumer demand for the product. Complete data are available on 398 out of the 450 manufacturing industries analyzed in the previous section. The price-cost margin and the rate of return on capital in hazardous and safe manufacturing industries, respectively, are exhibited in table 17, after adjusting for these other factors.[18] The influence of hazard-related industrial conflict is quite similar across the two measures. As the data in the first two rows of the table indicate, the rate of profit in hazardous industries was approximately 20% lower than the rate of profit in other industries that are comparable in terms of concentration, ease of entry, unionization, and changes in consumer demand, but that had safer working conditions.[19]

Table 17
Adjusted Percentage Rates of Profit in Hazardous and Safe Manufacturing Industries

	Hazardous Industries	Safe Industries	Ratio
All manufacturing			
Price-cost margin	6.3	7.7	0.81
Return on capital	31.5	38.1	0.83
Competitive sector			
Price-cost margin	6.0	8.0	0.75
Return on capital	30.6	38.8	0.79
Concentrated sector (excluding union effect)			
Price-cost margin	6.6	7.2	0.92
Return on capital	31.9	38.1	0.84
Concentrated sector (including union effect)			
Price-cost margin	6.3	7.5	0.84
Return on capital	31.3	38.7	0.81

Analogous price-cost margins and rates of return on capital for hazardous and safe industries within the competitive (unconcentrated) and concentrated sectors of manufacturing are also included in the table.[20] Profit rates were significantly lower in hazardous industries than in safe industries in both sectors. Within the competitive sector, the price-cost margin was 25% lower in hazardous than in safe industries, while the rate of return on capital was 21% lower. Within the concentrated sector, the price-cost margin was 8% lower in hazardous industries than in safe industries, while the rate of return on capital was 16% lower. This latter set of figures underrepresents the full association between injury rates and profit rates, since the profit data were already adjusted for the effects of labor unions. Consistent with other studies, these data indicate that unions significantly reduce profits in concentrated industries where implicit price collusion between firms is possible, but not in competitive industries. As shown in chapter 2, unions are much stronger in industries with high injury rates than in industries with low injury rates. Part of the adverse effect of injury rates on profits thus operates through the unions.

Profit rates in hazardous and safe industries, which have been adjusted for industry concentration, ease of entry, and consumer demand, but not for the extent of unionization, are presented in the final two rows of table 16. The observed influence of injury rates on profit rates is now larger. Hazardous working conditions were responsible for a 16% rather than an 8% difference in the price-cost margin, and a 19% rather than a 16% difference in the rate of return on capital. These hazard-related differences in profitability are still smaller than those observed in the competitive manufacturing sector.[21] The important point is that profit rates were lower in hazardous manufacturing industries than in safe ones during this period. Hazard-related industrial conflict during the 1970s contributed to the economic difficulties of that decade and helped stimulate management's subsequent efforts to reassert control.

Conclusion

Shop floor conflict between labor and management does not provide a workable long-term mechanism for controlling health and safety hazards. The economic costs of the production lost to absenteeism, slowdowns, and strikes are simply too great. Two quite different solutions are possible. First, management can recognize the legitimacy of labor's desire to participate in decision making concerning working conditions and other matters. This requires the recognition of union representation and the establishment of mechanisms to promote cooperative approaches to workplace problems. In countries that have adopted this approach, such as Sweden and Germany, occupational health is viewed as an area of labor-management cooperation. Workers enjoy extensive rights to be informed about hazards and to take precautionary steps to reduce exposures. Strikes are rare, however, and labor productivity levels are among the highest in the world.

The United States has not adopted this approach. Although the National Labor Relations Act of 1935 set the United States on a course similar to that followed by the social democratic nations of western Europe, management has subsequently chosen a second approach. This alternative rejects the principle of cooperation between equal partners and seeks to establish unquestioned managerial authority. Central to this approach is the elimination of union representation, a goal that has been pursued with tenacity and considerable success over the past thirty years. Getting rid of labor unions does not get rid of health and safety hazards, however, and American management has recognized the need to develop longer-term mechanisms for controlling workplace discontent. As will be discussed in chapter 8, some large employers have pioneered new "human resources" management techniques that facilitate a limited form of employee participation without union representation. Other sectors of management in the United States have looked to the past for ideas as to how to eliminate the need for worker participation. It is to the contemporary implementation of these traditional ideas that we now turn.

5

High Hazards and Low Wages

As workers come to recognize the risks posed by their jobs, they often join together to improve conditions. Nonunion workers in hazardous jobs are significantly more interested in union representation than are those in safe jobs, and labor unions are increasingly active in health and safety issues. Once unionized, workers seek improvements in wages and employment security as well as in health and safety. Over time, therefore, the successful pursuit of voice strategies produces a pattern in which undesirable job characteristics such as workplace hazards are balanced by other more desirable job characteristics. The unionized construction crafts and skilled production jobs in oil refineries, which typically pay high wages, exemplify this pattern.

Management does not remain passive in the face of worker efforts to improve hazardous jobs. The statistical evidence on discharges, strikes, and productivity losses in hazardous industries testifies to the intensity of this resistance. Shop floor conflict is extremely expensive, motivating management to develop longer-term strategies for controlling costs. The steep decline in union representation reflects the success of management's efforts to eliminate worker-controlled institutions from the labor market. More important, management has sought to organize the process of production in many hazardous industries so as to reduce the need for highly skilled workers. To the extent possible, management replaces these workers with a combination of less skilled employees and increased supervision and control. Over time, managerial responses produce a pattern in which hazardous jobs require less educational achievement, provide less on-the-job training, and offer fewer opportunities for worker autonomy, responsibility, and creativity in the work process. These unskilled hazardous jobs pay lower wages than skilled safe jobs.

This chapter, which focuses on educational requirements, on-the-job training, decision-making authority, employee autonomy, employment security, and wages, examines the longer-term consequences of worker and management efforts to control hazardous jobs. It provides another vantage point from which to evaluate the strengths and weaknesses of private worker strategies to reduce health and safety hazards. To the extent that worker voice strategies are successful, we expect to find that hazardous jobs pay high wages and offer other desirable features that compensate workers for the risks they face. To the extent that management efforts to forestall voice strategies and reduce skill requirements are successful, however, we expect to find that hazardous jobs pay low wages and offer few compensating features.

Compensating Differentials and Noncompeting Groups in the Labor Market

The most famous theory of how social forces influence job characteristics was developed over 200 years ago by the Scottish economist Adam Smith and has come to be known as the theory of compensating differentials. In his book, *The Wealth of Nations*, published in 1776, Smith claimed that labor market competition forces employers whose jobs are hazardous to offer higher wages or some other desirable feature to attract employees. If these inducements are not offered, Smith argued, workers will simply refuse to enter hazardous occupations. While particular jobs may differ as to the kind of working conditions they offer, the overall value of the employments will be approximately equal in the eyes of the workers. Jobs rating poorly on some measures of quality will rate well on other measures. As Smith himself explains:

> The whole of the advantages and disadvantages of the different employments of labour and stock [capital] must, in the same neighborhood, be either perfectly equal or continually tending to equality. If in the same neighborhood there was any employment evidently either more or less advantageous than the rest, so many people would crowd into it in the one case, and so many would desert it in the other, that its advantage would soon return to the level of other employments.[1]

These competitive pressures have significant consequences. First, extra wages compensate workers for the extra risks they face. Hazard pay acts as a sort of insurance premium, paid by the employer to all employees, of which only some subsequently suffer the event for which the insurance is provided. Second, and of equal importance, hazard pay premiums provide employers with incentives to reduce health and safety risks. Up to a certain point, investments in safety protections can be recouped in the form of reduced wage premiums. Competition between workers in the labor market thus provides compensation for injured workers and incentives for prevention of new injuries.

Two assumptions underlie Adam Smith's theory of compensating differentials. First, workers must be aware of the hazards they face and must not adopt an attitude of complacency, denial, or machismo. Second, workers must have a number of meaningful job possibilities. Both of these assumptions are at variance with the facts in the real world. Workers are often not aware of the risks they face; this is particularly true in the case of subtle, long-term hazards to health. The number of realistic job options enjoyed by different workers varies widely depending on their skills and social status. To the extent that hazardous occupations are filled with less skilled and socially disadvantaged workers, Adam Smith's theory implies that they will offer only meager hazard pay premiums.

Even given its limitations, however, the theory of compensating differentials is a first step toward understanding the clustering of job characteristics. While workers are unaware of some of the health and safety hazards they face on the job, they are aware of many others. Risk of injuries, which occur frequently and are often linked visibly to their causes, may be reasonably well understood. As illustrated in the DBCP case, some workers also recognize long-term health hazards. While access to job alternatives differs among workers, it is very hard to argue that workers have no choices as to where they can work. Quitting a hazardous job in a chemical factory may require a worker to take a low-paying job in a restaurant or gas station, for example, but this is precisely the choice between wages and safety that is the focus of Adam Smith's theory of compensating differentials.

The most famous alternative to Adam Smith's theory is the theory of noncompeting groups, originally developed by John Stuart Mill in the middle of the nineteenth century. For Mill, the theory of compensating differentials was outrageously at odds with day-to-day observations about the wages paid in jobs with bad working conditions. In *The Principles of Political Economy*, published in 1848, Mill comments directly on Smith's theory:

> These inequalities of remuneration, which are supposed to compensate for the disagreeable circumstances of particular employments, would, under certain conditions, be natural consequences of perfectly free competition; and as between employments of about the same grade, and filled by nearly the same description of people, they are, no doubt, for the most part, realized in practice. But it is altogether a false view of the state of the facts, to present this as the relation which generally exists between agreeable and disagreeable employments. The really exhausting and the really repulsive labours, instead of being better paid than others, are almost invariably paid the worst of all, because performed by those who have no choice. . . . The more revolting the occupation,

the more certain it is to receive the minimum of remuneration, because it devolves on the most helpless and degraded, on those who from squalid poverty, or from want of skill and education, are rejected from all other employments.[2]

Mill focuses here on the level of skill demanded in hazardous jobs and on the type of worker usually employed there. He agrees with Smith that hazard pay premiums would be observed when comparing dangerous and safe jobs that require similar skill levels and are staffed by similar workers. He emphasizes, however, that hazardous and safe jobs tend to differ in skill requirements and work-force characteristics as well as in risk to life and limb. When just comparing wage rates across jobs, not adjusting for skill requirements, one observes that hazardous jobs pay substantially less than safe jobs.

If hazardous jobs pay lower wages than safe jobs, as the theory of noncompeting groups claims, it must be because employers using hazardous technologies have been able to organize the production process in a way that avoids the need for skilled workers. The expedient way to hold down wage rates is to hold down skill requirements. Of course, unskilled workers are less productive than are skilled workers. All employers seek the appropriate balance of skills, productivity, and wages that yields the highest surplus of revenues over costs. Some employers find that the greater productivity of skilled workers more than covers the higher wages they demand, and so develop a process of production that relies on worker skills. Other employers find that the extra productivity of skilled workers is not adequate to cover their wage demands, and develop a process of production that relies heavily on automation and supervisory authority rather than on worker skills.

John Stuart Mill's theory of noncompeting groups implies that employers using hazardous technologies generally select the latter option, reducing skill requirements and wage rates rather than raising them. Skilled workers require higher hazard pay premiums than unskilled workers. The additional wages associated with exposure to a particular health or safety hazard will be higher for employers using skilled workers who have many job options than for employers using unskilled workers who have few options. Employers thus find that it is more profitable to use less productive but lower-paid unskilled workers for jobs posing health and safety risks.[3]

Adam Smith and John Stuart Mill emphasize two quite different features of the economy. For Smith, the important feature of the labor market is its competitive nature. In contrast to the labor market in feudal European societies, vestiges of which remained in Smith's time, workers in a capitalist labor market are free to move between occupations according to the relative advantages and disadvantages of these occupations. Workers with equal skills are treated equally. For Mill, on the other hand, the important characteristic of modern society is the inequality in access to education and training that persists among workers. While labor markets treat similar workers equally, they treat dissimilar workers unequally.

Educational Requirements

The 1977 Quality of Employment Survey and the 1978 and 1980 National Longitudinal Surveys, already used in previous chapters, ask a number of questions concerning job and worker characteristics. Since the two surveys also contain information on each respondent's occupation, the workers can be divided into two groups according to the level of health and safety hazard they face. The average level of skill required and wages paid can be calculated separately for workers in hazardous occupations and for workers in safe occupations, and then the two averages can be compared.[4]

The classification of individual workers as employed in hazardous or safe occupations is obviously central to the statistical analysis. The U.S. Bureau of Labor Statistics has developed an index of risk for each occupation based on 1978 Workers' Compensation claims data from twenty-five states.[5] Occupations with rates of injury and illness above the economywide average are defined as hazardous for present purposes. Conversely, occupations with below-average rates of claims are defined as safe. This measure of risk was used to avoid the limitations of both the subjective worker-reported measures of exposure and the industry injury rate, which have been used for other purposes in previous chapters. Subjective worker perceptions of hazard exposure are undesirable here since it is possible that individuals dissatisfied with other characteristics of their jobs will be more likely to describe those jobs as hazardous than will generally satisfied workers employed in the very same jobs. Industry injury rates do not reflect differences in risks faced by different occupations within the same industry, such as by laborers and secretaries in the mining industry.

The different levels of education attained by QES and NLS interviewees in hazardous and safe occupations are illustrated in table 18. The levels of education represented are less

Table 18
*Percentage of Workers at Each Level of Education
in Hazardous and Safe Occupations*

Education Level	Hazardous Occupations	Safe Occupations	Ratio
Fewer than 12 years			
1977 QES	35.3	13.4	2.63
1978–80 NLS	28.7	9.2	3.12
High school diploma			
1977 QES	44.9	31.0	1.45
1978–80 NLS	44.4	32.5	1.37
Some college			
1977 QES	16.9	26.2	0.65
1978–80 NLS	18.2	22.0	0.83
College diploma			
1977 QES	2.9	29.4	0.09
1978–80 NLS	8.7	36.3	0.24

than twelve years, high school diploma, some college course-
work but no four-year college degree, and a four-year college
diploma or more. While these data reflect educational
achievements by workers rather than educational requirements for jobs, the two are closely associated, and achievements can be used as a reasonable measure of requirements.
The association between hazard levels and educational requirements is very powerful. While approximately one-third
of workers in hazardous occupations lack a high school diploma, only one-tenth of workers in safe occupations have no
diploma. At the other end of the educational spectrum the
percentages are reversed. While 30–35% of workers in safe occupations graduated from a four-year college program, less
than 10% of workers in hazardous occupations have a college
diploma.

On-the-Job Training and Promotions

Most firms offer more than one type of job. Each position is often connected to other jobs by transfer or promotion possibilities. In order to move up the job ladder into more pleasant,
challenging, and highly paid positions, workers often need to
acquire new skills. This is typically done on the job. Indeed,
many firms have highly structured "internal labor markets,"
where each job is assigned a position in a promotion sequence. Workers who successfully master the tasks required
in one position are eligible for promotion to the next job in
their sequence. Blue-collar as well as white-collar workers
may enjoy possibilities for careers composed of jobs of increasing desirability.

Hazardous occupations may be tolerable if they are linked
with more desirable jobs within promotion sequences. It
might be viewed as equitable for unsafe jobs to be assigned to
newly hired workers if those workers have access to safer jobs
as they accumulate training and seniority. If, on the other
hand, hazardous occupations were cut off from more desir-

able occupations, then they would indeed be dead-end positions relegated to workers who have the fewest job choices.
Hazardous occupations can be segregated from safe occupations in either of two ways. Within firms, hazardous jobs
could be assigned to shorter job ladders, with transfer to
longer and more desirable ladders restricted by the rules of
the internal labor market. Alternatively, hazardous occupations could be concentrated in firms and industries that do
not offer the type of on-the-job training necessary to move to
safer firms and industries.

The percentages of workers in the QES and NLS surveys
who describe their jobs as offering no valuable on-the-job
training and poor promotion possibilities are exhibited in table 19.[6] Workers in hazardous occupations are considerably
less likely to receive on-the-job training than workers in safe
occupations. While only 10% of QES interviewees in safe jobs
report receiving no on-the-job training, 26% of those in hazardous jobs report a lack of such training. Within the NLS
group, workers in hazardous occupations were 50% more

Table 19
*Percentage of Workers Describing Possibilities for On-the-Job
Training and Promotion in Hazardous and Safe Occupations*

	Hazardous Occupations	*Safe Occupations*	*Ratio*
Workers reporting no valuable skills are learned			
1977 QES	26.4	10.0	2.64
1978–80 NLS	36.4	24.6	1.48
Workers reporting promotion chances are poor			
1977 QES	62.8	52.9	1.19
1978–80 NLS	51.6	49.6	1.04

likely than workers in safe occupations to report they lack on-the-job training. Compared to workers in safe occupations, workers in hazardous occupations more often report a lack of promotion possibilities, although the differences were smaller than in the case of on-the-job training. QES workers are 19% more likely to report the absence of meaningful promotion possibilities if they are employed in hazardous occupations than if they are employed in safe occupations. Among NLS interviewees, the hazard-related difference is only 4%.

Job Content and Worker Autonomy

The QES asked workers about both the nature of the tasks they performed and the extent to which the workers themselves controlled the manner, sequence, and pace at which the tasks are performed.[7] We focus here on the workers' answers to the broadest set of questions, which indicate whether they considered their jobs to be (1) uncreative, (2) monotonous, or (3) meaningless.[8] The extent of worker autonomy and control is measured using responses to the questions as to whether the worker lacked significant control over (4) the content of job duties, (5) the pace of work, or (6) the hours of work, and finally, (7) whether the "job has rules and regulations governing everything [the worker] might do or say."[9]

The percentages of QES workers who report various job characteristics are arranged according to hazardous and safe occupations in table 20. The pattern of responses is striking. For each of the seven questions, workers in more hazardous occupations are more likely to characterize their job in a negative light than workers in safe occupations. Workers in hazardous occupations are 50–190% more likely than workers in safe occupations to describe their jobs as uncreative, monotonous, meaningless, and as providing no worker control over work pace. They are 10–20% more likely to report no control over job duties, no control over work hours, and the pervasiveness of rules.

Table 20
Percentage of Workers Describing Job Content and Worker Autonomy in Hazardous and Safe Occupations

QES Workers Reporting	Hazardous Occupations	Safe Occupations	Ratio
Uncreative work	52.6	27.7	1.90
Monotonous work	23.5	8.2	2.87
Meaningless work	12.0	6.9	1.74
No control over work duties	58.0	49.7	1.17
No control over work pace	23.1	15.1	1.53
No control over work hours	24.8	22.9	1.08
Rules governing everything	50.6	46.2	1.10

Job Security and Layoffs

However unsafe, monotonous, and unrewarding their jobs may be, workers do not like to lose them unexpectedly. Job security is one of the main concerns of workers in the U.S. economy. Loss of a job can entail an immediate decline in the worker's standard of living. If the worker does not find an equivalent position within a relatively short period of time, job loss can cause serious long-term changes in life-style and well-being. Long-term unemployment is often associated with mental anxiety, family problems, and a range of self-destructive behaviors.

The measures of job security in hazardous and safe employments presented in table 21 derive from four nationally representative sources of data. In addition to figures provided by the QES and NLS, numbers are drawn from the 1974 and 1985 years of the Panel Study of Income Dynamics and from manufacturing firms surveyed by the U.S. Bureau of Labor Statistics in 1977.[10] These data offer four distinct measures of employment security. The QES and NLS asked workers if they considered job security to be poor.[11] The QES, in addition, asked workers if they expected to be permanently laid off over

Table 21
Percentage of Workers Describing Job Security and Suffering Layoffs in Hazardous and Safe Occupations

	Hazardous Occupations	Safe Occupations	Ratio
Workers viewing their jobs as insecure			
1977 QES	24.4	20.6	1.18
1978–80 NLS	30.9	21.5	1.44
Workers expecting to be permanently laid off in next few years			
1977 QES	17.9	13.4	1.34
Workers losing their jobs due to permanent layoff			
1977 BLS	3.2	1.9	1.68
1978–80 NLS	10.3	3.7	2.78
1974 PSID	6.2	2.9	2.14
1985 PSID	5.9	3.6	1.64
Workers temporarily laid off			
1977 BLS	11.1	4.7	2.36

the next few years.[12] Actual rates of permanent layoffs, as distinct from layoff expectations, are available in the NLS, PSID, and BLS data. The NLS reinterviews the same workers every two years and asks whether they have suffered permanent layoffs in the interval between interviews. The PSID asks similar questions each year. The BLS survey queries employers in manufacturing firms concerning the percentage of their workers who were temporarily and permanently laid off over the course of each year.[13]

The figures in table 21 are unequivocal. In each of the four data sources and for each of the four measures of job security, hazardous occupations offer significantly less employment security than do safe occupations. QES and NLS workers in hazardous occupations are 18–44% more likely to describe their jobs as generally insecure than workers in safe occupations. QES interviewees are 34% more likely to report layoff expectations if they work in hazardous occupations than if they work in safe occupations. Rates of permanent layoffs range from 64% to 178% higher in hazardous occupations than in safe occupations.[14] Rates of temporary layoffs in hazardous manufacturing industries are over twice as high as those in safe manufacturing industries.[15]

Hourly Wages and Annual Earnings

The wage rate is often the most important characteristic of a job from the worker's point of view, since it determines the worker's life-style. The vast majority of people in the United States depend on wages rather than earnings off stocks, bonds, and other investments for their needs. The wage rate is also typically the job characteristic that is most visible and most useful for comparing alternative positions. The wages in hazardous and safe occupations are thus the best index of comparison for the two employments.

Measures of earnings are available in all four of the data sources used earlier and from one additional source. The NLS and PSID asked respondents for the hourly wage they were paid and, for those workers paid on a weekly or monthly basis, calculated average hourly wages using information on hours worked. Unfortunately, the QES did not obtain the information on hours worked necessary to compute average hourly wages. It does, however, report each worker's annual earnings. The BLS manufacturing data report the average hourly wages for industry employees. Hourly wage data are also available for workers responding to the Current Population Survey, the large monthly survey used to measure trends in union representation in chapter 2. This source offers a long series of worker-specific data covering the 1968–86 period.

Average hourly wages and annual earnings for workers in hazardous and safe occupations are recorded in table 22. The pattern across the various data sets is consistent and clear: workers in hazardous occupations are paid less than workers in safe occupations. Among CPS respondents, the largest sample of workers represented here, the average wage paid in hazardous occupations in the late 1960s was only 77% of that paid in safe occupations. This ratio rose to 81% by 1977 but then fell again to 69% by 1986. The BLS, PSID, and QES data consistently report wages in hazardous occupations as 20% below wages in safe occupations. The NLS is somewhat different, reporting wages in hazardous occupations as only 5% lower than those in safe occupations.

The pattern of job characteristics in hazardous and safe occupations leaves no doubt as to the general quality of hazardous occupations. Compared with safe occupations, hazardous occupations require less formal education and offer less on-

Table 22
Hourly Wages and Annual Earnings
in Hazardous and Safe Occupations
(in Dollars)

	Hazardous Occupations	Safe Occupations	Ratio
Hourly wages			
1968 CPS	3.29	4.25	0.77
1977 CPS	5.10	6.32	0.81
1986 CPS	7.95	11.49	0.69
1977 BLS	5.32	6.69	0.80
1978–80 NLS	6.11	6.40	0.95
1974 PSID	4.68	5.86	0.80
1985 PSID	9.28	10.86	0.85
Annual earnings			
1977 QES	12,583	14,669	0.86

the-job training and promotion possibilities. Hazardous occupations are more monotonous, more narrowly defined, and more frequently governed by rules and regulations. Compared with safe occupations, they pose greater risks of temporary and permanent layoffs and offer lower wages. The statistical data underline the acuity of John Stuart Mill's insight concerning unsafe jobs. The typical hazardous occupation is unattractive in virtually every measurable dimension. People clearly do not voluntarily choose hazardous occupations if they have other possibilities.

Testing the Hazard Pay Hypothesis

The general association between hazards and wages across occupations in the U.S. economy, which is documented by the data gathered in table 22, proves that unsafe jobs are generally lower-paying than safe jobs. These findings do not, however, directly test the theory of compensating differentials as developed by Adam Smith. That theory argues that pay levels are higher in hazardous than in safe jobs, but only after one adjusts for skill levels and other factors influencing wages.

The QES and NLS provide job and worker-specific measures of risk of occupational injury and illness. Respondents to those surveys were asked questions concerning the working conditions in their jobs including questions regarding various types of health and safety hazards. The answers to these questions obviously represent the workers' subjective evaluations of the hazards rather than the sort of evaluation that would be made by a safety engineer or industrial hygienist. Nevertheless, they are useful for our purposes. They are specific to each worker's individual job, rather than relating to the worker's occupation as a whole. The subjective nature of the measures is an advantage here. If labor market competition is to generate wage premiums in hazardous jobs, this must occur in those jobs where the workers themselves are aware of the hazards. If a job is hazardous but the workers are unaware of this fact, there is no need for the employer to pay a wage premium in order to keep the employees on the job.

Three hazard measures will be used here to test the theory of compensating differentials, one concerning worker perceptions of safety hazards, a second concerning perceptions of health hazards, and a third concerning perceptions of exposure to either safety or health hazards. QES workers are considered to perceive their jobs as posing safety hazards if they report "sizeable" or "great" problems due to exposure to (1) "dangers from fire, burn, or shock"; (2) "dangerous tools, machinery, or equipment"; (3) "dangerous work methods"; or (4) "risk of traffic accidents while working." They perceive their jobs as unhealthy if they report "sizeable" or "great" problems due to exposure to (1) "dangerous chemicals"; (2) "air pollution from dust, smoke, gas, fumes, fibers, or other things"; or (3) "risk of catching disease." NLS workers perceive safety hazards if they strongly agree that "the job is dangerous" and health hazards if they strongly agree that they are "exposed to unhealthy conditions."

In order to obtain evidence of hazard pay premiums for each specific job, it will be necessary to statistically adjust for as many other determinants of wage rates as possible. Differences in wages across the economy are due to three broad categories of influences. The first concerns worker skills and aptitudes, plus the effects of discrimination. The QES and NLS include information on each respondent's race, sex, years of education, years of seniority on the job, and age, which together account for many of the most obvious differences in skill levels and the potential for discrimination. The second set of influences on wage rates concerns job characteristics, including hazards. The theory of compensating differentials argues that all undesirable job characteristics, not just health and safety risks, should receive wage compensation. It will be important to control for as many of these attributes as possible in order to distinguish the independent influence of workplace hazards themselves on wage rates. In order to make the

QES and NLS data as comparable as possible, the analyses are statistically adjusted for those job attributes that are measured in both surveys: availability of training possibilities, availability of promotion possibilities, extent of employment security, whether the physical surroundings are pleasant, and whether the worker considers his or her supervisor to be competent. The analysis also adjusts for whether the job is unionized, since labor unions tend to raise wages for their members. The analysis is limited to blue-collar workers in order to ensure the comparability of unmeasured job characteristics. The third and final set of influences on wage rates concerns geographical differences in the cost of living. Firms in high-cost areas must pay higher wages than firms in low-cost areas in order to obtain the same supply of labor. The analysis is adjusted for whether each QES and NLS worker resides in an urban or rural area and also for the region of the nation in which the worker lives.[16]

Annual earnings and hourly wages for QES and NLS workers in hazardous and safe jobs are displayed in table 23. These figures are adjusted for worker and job differences in skills, demographic attributes, working conditions aside from hazards, and the area cost of living. Consistent with the theory of compensating differentials, pay levels are higher in jobs where workers report serious risks than in jobs not posing such risks. Blue-collar QES workers earned $318 more in 1977 if they faced "sizeable" or "great" occupational hazards than if they did not face such hazards. This represents a 3% premium over wages earned in safe jobs. NLS workers reporting serious hazards earned an average differential of 40 cents per hour, 7% above the wages earned by comparable workers in safer jobs. This is equivalent to an annual premium of $800 for NLS workers employed full-time throughout the entire year. The 3–7% range in hazard pay premiums reported here is consistent with findings of other economic studies of compensating differentials.[17] The wage premiums, while modest in size, do demonstrate the influence of worker preferences for safe over hazardous working conditions and the resulting

Table 23
Annual Earnings and Hourly Wages in Hazardous and
Safe Jobs, After Adjusting for Other Job Characteristics
(in Dollars)

	Hazardous Jobs	Safe Jobs	Ratio
Either safety or health hazard			
1977 QES (annual earnings)	12,013	11,695	1.03
1978–80 NLS (hourly wages)	6.45	6.05	1.07
Safety hazard			
1977 QES (annual earnings)	12,235	11,623	1.05
1978–80 NLS (hourly wages)	6.55	6.05	1.08
Health hazard			
1977 QES (annual earnings)	12,113	11,711	1.03
1978–80 NLS (hourly wages)	6.30	6.25	1.01

necessity for employers offering hazardous jobs to compensate their employees.

The degree of compensation for exposure to occupational hazards depends on the nature of the exposure, as data in the third through sixth rows of table 23 indicate. Disaggregation of the overall wage-hazard relationship into safety hazards and health hazards reveals that modest premiums were paid to workers exposed to safety hazards, but not to those exposed to health hazards. Blue-collar QES and NLS workers exposed to significant risks of on-the-job injury received wage premiums amounting to 5% and 8%, respectively, above the earnings of blue-collar workers not exposed to injury risks. Workers exposed to occupational health hazards earned 1–3% more than comparable workers not exposed to those hazards, but these small differences are not statistically significant.

Conclusion

Workers in hazardous occupations face a variety of risks to their health and safety. Sudden exertions or an unprotected cutting blade can knock them off the job for a week or three months and sometimes leave permanent impairments that limit the kind of work they can perform in the future. Chemical exposures can lead to cancer, diseases of the nervous system, or birth defects in their children. Workers in health-care settings are exposed to hepatitis, AIDS, and other infectious diseases.

As documented in this chapter, however, risks to life and limb are not the only undesirable features of hazardous occupations. Hazardous occupations require less education and offer less on-the-job training and fewer promotion possibilities than do safe occupations. These employments are often monotonous and boring, empty of meaning to the worker, and governed by rigid rules and regulations. While modest wage premiums are paid to workers exposed to hazards within particular occupations and industries, the general pattern of wages and working conditions reveals that hazardous employments pay wages 20–30% less than safe employments.

This clustering of undesirable job characteristics must be interpreted in light of the data presented in previous chapters on worker responses to workplace hazards. At first glance, the fact that hazardous jobs pay low wages and offer few possibilities for worker participation and control might appear to conflict with the evidence that workers are aware of many hazards and pursue exit and voice strategies to obtain safer conditions. The clustering of undesirable job characteristics might be understood as support for a view of workers as ignorant and apathetic concerning workplace hazards. Nothing could be farther from the truth. If workers were unaware of or unconcerned about occupational hazards, we would find no particular association between the health and safety risk posed by particular jobs and the other characteristics of those jobs. It is precisely because workers are aware of many occupational hazards and do respond to those hazards that we observe clustering of undesirable job characteristics. Workers with good job options generally avoid hazardous positions and demand wage premiums for those risks they face. Employers, however, respond to demands for compensating differentials by reducing skill requirements and then lowering wages rather than raising them. Endemic social and economic inequality in society at large provides these employers with a supply of disadvantaged workers willing to accept health and safety risks in return for very modest amounts of compensation.

6

Racial Inequality and the Logic of the Labor Market

Hazardous jobs are lousy jobs. Compared to safe employments, they require fewer skills and offer less on-the-job training, allow less worker autonomy and control, pose greater
threats of layoff and discharge, and pay lower wages. In some
instances, collective worker and labor union efforts have been
successful in combating this pattern, raising wages and improving job security. The rarity of these exceptions to the labor market rule testifies to the strength of management and
the weakness of unions in the U.S. economy. This pattern of
high hazards and low wages requires further explanation,
however. Even if voice strategies have often proven ineffective
in improving the quality of hazardous jobs, why have not exit
strategies by individual workers raised wages in those jobs? If
hazardous occupations pay less, who would choose to work
there?

The pattern of hazards and wages in the U.S. economy
could not exist without a large supply of socially disadvantaged workers willing to accept both high hazards and low
wages. In an egalitarian society, worker mobility and labor
market competition would produce a pattern in which hazardous jobs paid higher wages than safe jobs. An egalitarian
labor force would insist upon an egalitarian occupational
structure in which jobs with undesirable features exhibited
offsetting desirable features. But this is not the world we live in.

A nation of immigrants, the United States has been able to count upon an ever-replenished supply of workers willing to accept the dirtiest and most dangerous jobs as their rite of passage into American society. Immigrants' children have typically done better than their parents, learning the language and gaining the skills needed to move to safer and more lucrative pursuits, and leaving the backbreaking work for the next generation of immigrants. This process continues today, with the rapid influx of young workers from Mexico, Central America, and other parts of the developing world. There is one salient exception. Black Americans, descendants of involuntary immigrants, have experienced difficulty in escaping from the lowest strata of the labor market. Racist attitudes and institutions have combined to block many of the traditional paths leading out of the risky trades. Only in recent decades has American society made a serious effort to undo the effects of centuries of discrimination and equalize labor market opportunities for black workers.

This chapter examines the ethnic mix of workers employed in hazardous jobs and compares this to the mix of workers in safe jobs. It looks at exposure to different types of occupational injuries and illnesses and how these are distributed among black, Hispanic, and non-Hispanic white Americans. The focus then shifts to trends in hazardous exposures, as a means of evaluating the impact of governmental programs to reduce racial inequality. Trends in exposure to occupational safety and health hazards are also compared with trends in unemployment and wages. The chapter concludes with an evaluation of the manner in which a market economy shifts the greatest burden of work-related disability onto the least advantaged members of the working class.

Ethnic Differences in Exposure to Workplace Hazards

Rates of work-related injury and acute illness for black, Hispanic, and non-Hispanic white workers in 1986 are portrayed

Table 24
*Ethnic Differences in Rates of Occupational Injury and
Acute Illness per 1,000 Male Workers, California, 1986*

	Black Workers	Hispanic Workers	White Workers	B/W Ratio	H/W Ratio
Total illnesses and injuries	53.4	67.5	37.7	1.42	1.79
Acute illnesses	3.7	4.0	2.9	1.28	1.38
Crushing injuries	4.5	5.7	2.9	1.55	1.97
Cuts and punctures	6.3	10.2	5.2	1.21	1.96
Abrasions	1.7	3.0	1.5	1.13	2.00
Bone fractures	5.1	7.0	4.0	1.28	1.75
Strains and sprains	24.5	28.3	16.0	1.53	1.85

in tables 24 and 25. These data are derived from the California Workers' Compensation reporting system, which annually publishes counts of each major type of injury and illness in each occupation. When combined with census information on occupational employment for each ethnic group, these data allow insights into differences in risks faced at work by the three groups.[1]

The rate of disabling occupational events, combining all types of injuries and illnesses, was almost 7% in 1986 (67.5 per 1,000) for Hispanic men, over 5% (53.4 per 1,000) for black men, and less than 4% (37.7 per 1,000) for white men, as the data in the first row of table 24 testify. Hispanic men were thus 80% more likely to suffer a disabling injury or illness than whites, while black men were 40% more likely. Injury and illness rates were lower among women than among men for all groups, but strong ethnic differences were found there also. As the data in the first row of table 25 demonstrate, Hispanic women were almost 60% more likely than their white coworkers and black women were almost 40% more likely than their white coworkers to suffer a disabling injury or illness.

Table 25
Ethnic Differences in Rates of Occupational Injury and
Acute Illness per 1,000 Female Workers, California, 1986

	Black Workers	Hispanic Workers	White Workers	B/W Ratio	H/W Ratio
Total illnesses and injuries	28.8	32.8	21.0	1.37	1.56
Acute illnesses	2.7	2.4	2.0	1.35	1.20
Crushing injuries	2.3	3.0	1.7	1.35	1.76
Cuts and punctures	2.5	4.2	2.3	1.09	1.83
Abrasions	0.5	0.8	0.4	1.25	2.00
Bone fractures	2.4	2.8	1.9	1.26	1.47
Strains and sprains	14.2	14.7	9.5	1.50	1.55

Ethnic differences in exposure to occupational hazards varied by the type of hazard. Among Hispanic workers, risks were especially high for crushing injuries, cuts and punctures, and abrasions, while for blacks risks were high for strains and sprains. Ethnic differences in occupational illnesses were somewhat narrower than were differences in occupational injuries. Occupational illness includes a very heterogeneous set of problems. In order of relative frequency, occupational illnesses reported to the California Workers' Compensation system include diseases of the circulatory system; systemic poisoning; anxiety and mental disorders; dermatitis; eye disease; infective and parasitic disease; inflammation and irritation of bones, joints, tendons, or muscles; radiation effects, including welder's flash; and serum and toxic hepatitis.[2]

Trends in Exposure Differences

The past thirty years have witnessed a broad effort by private organizations and public institutions to reduce the effects of racial discrimination. The civil rights movement of the 1950s and 1960s focused on explicit forms of racial segregation in housing, services, and employment. Equal opportunity and affirmative action programs since the 1960s have targeted more subtle forms of discrimination. The most important changes have occurred quietly, as racist sentiment among whites has gradually diminished, albeit with occasional virulent flare-ups.[3] An obvious and important question is whether these efforts to reduce racial inequality have produced meaningful benefits for blacks.

To obtain insights into trends in ethnic differences, two approaches are possible. The first examines exposures as reported by workers and is able to distinguish perceived risks of illness from perceived risks of injury. Various surveys of workers conducted over the past twenty-five years ask questions concerning exposure to health and safety risks on the job. These surveys differ somewhat but are similar enough for purposes of comparison. The second approach uses actual injury and acute illness rates rather than perceived exposure to risks and complements the analysis of worker risk perceptions by focusing on the outcome of the exposures. Its disadvantage lies in the exclusion of long-term health effects.

The first approach, which focuses on perceived exposures, is embodied in the data collected in tables 26 and 27. The percentages of male workers who report occupational health and safety hazards in four surveys spanning the period from 1967 to 1984 are featured in table 26. The 1977 Quality of Employment Survey, the 1978 National Longitudinal Survey, and the 1984 AFL-CIO Louis Harris survey have been used in previous chapters. The data from the 1967 Survey of Economic Opportunity (SEO) were obtained from a published study that examined a range of job characteristics.[4] These surveys permit an analysis of differences in exposure to hazards for blacks and whites. Hispanic workers were not distinguished from non-Hispanic whites and thus are included with other whites in these four surveys. One salient difference between these surveys should be noted. As discussed in previous chapters, the QES, NLS, and AFL surveys report the worker's own perceptions of exposure to hazard. In contrast, the SEO was

Table 26
*Percentage of Male Workers Exposed to Occupational Safety
and Health Hazards, 1967–1984*

	Black Workers	White Workers	B/W Ratio
Any health or safety hazard			
1967 SEO	45.1	36.3	1.24
1977 QES	54.5	41.2	1.32
1978 NLS	53.8	39.9	1.35
1984 AFL	64.8	44.4	1.46
Any health hazard			
1967 SEO	23.2	14.5	1.60
1977 QES	36.5	20.2	1.81
1978 NLS	33.8	25.4	1.33
1984 AFL	—	—	—
Any safety hazard			
1967 SEO	27.5	21.6	1.27
1977 QES	28.8	28.5	1.01
1978 NLS	41.2	30.1	1.37
1984 AFL	—	—	—

linked to data from the Dictionary of Occupational Titles
(DOT). The DOT was developed to help young people make informed career choices, and contains a wide range of information on each occupation. The hazard exposure information is
not based on evaluations by health and safety professionals,
but by job evaluators with no formal health and safety training. In this sense the SEO data are analogous to the worker
perceptions of hazard reported in the QES, NLS, and AFL surveys.

The percentage of male workers reporting any safety or
health hazard rose steadily throughout this period, from 45%
among blacks and 36% among whites in 1967 up to 65%
among blacks and 44% among whites in 1984. Exposure grew

more rapidly for blacks than for whites. While blacks were 20% more likely to report an occupational hazard than whites in 1967, they were 50% more likely to do so in 1984. Perceptions of health and safety hazards for 1967–78 are portrayed separately in the second and third sections of the table. Unfortunately, the 1984 survey did not include separate data on health and safety hazards. The percentage of male workers reporting health hazards rose from 23% among blacks and 15% among whites in 1967 to 34% among blacks and 25% among whites in 1978. Perceived exposure to safety hazards rose from 28% among blacks and 22% among whites in 1967 to 41% among blacks and 30% among whites during this ten-year period. The excess of black exposure over white exposure narrowed from 60% to 30% for health hazards but increased slightly from 30% to 40% for safety hazards.

Analogous exposure perceptions for female workers over the 1967 to 1984 period are documented in table 27. The percentage of women reporting any safety or health hazard on the job increased from 31% among blacks and 16% among whites in 1967 to 36% among blacks and 32% among whites in 1984. In contrast to the exposure trends for men, racial differentials declined among women, from a 90% increased risk for blacks in 1967 to a 27% increased risk in 1980. This decline in racial differentials occurred for both perceived health hazards (90% in 1967 to 20% in 1980) and perceived safety hazards (110% in 1967 to 40% in 1980).

The exposure perception data included in tables 26 and 27 permit assessments of the working conditions faced in different years by different groups of workers, but they shed no direct light on whether those working conditions actually resulted in adverse outcomes. Data on work-related injuries and acute illnesses are available, however, and can be linked to demographic data on the workers employed in particular occupations.

The Current Population Survey and the Panel Study of Income Dynamics have been analyzed in previous chapters. For present purposes it is important to emphasize one difference

Table 27
Percentage of Female Workers Exposed to Occupational Safety and Health Hazards, 1967–1984

	Black Workers	White Workers	B/W Ratio
Any health or safety hazard			
1967 SEO	31.1	16.1	1.93
1977 QES	40.0	29.3	1.37
1980 NLS	31.6	24.9	1.27
1984 AFL	35.8	31.6	1.13
Any health hazard			
1967 SEO	15.9	8.3	1.92
1977 QES	30.5	16.2	1.88
1980 NLS	22.5	18.8	1.20
1984 AFL	—	—	—
Any safety hazard			
1967 SEO	13.2	6.4	2.06
1977 QES	16.7	13.2	1.27
1980 NLS	17.3	12.0	1.44
1984 AFL	—	—	—

between them. The CPS interviews different individuals in different years, while the PSID reinterviews the same individuals year after year. The cross-sectional CPS can be interpreted as offering a series of "snapshots" of the U.S. working population, while the longitudinal PSID offers a "movie" of the experiences of one group of workers.[5] The number of workers interviewed in the two surveys also differs considerably. Depending on the year, the CPS contains responses from 20,000 to 34,000 men and from 12,000 to 31,000 women, while the PSID covers approximately 4,500 workers in each year. The CPS data are available from 1968 to 1986, while the PSID data are limited to 1971 through 1985. Both surveys contain detailed information on the industry in which each respondent is employed. This employment information can be linked

Table 28
*Percentage of Male Workers Suffering a Disabling Occupational
Injury or Acute Illness, 1968–1986*

	Black Workers	White Workers	B/W Ratio
Current Population Survey (CPS)			
1968	5.7	3.2	1.78
1977	8.3	5.2	1.60
1986	6.5	4.6	1.41
Panel Study of Income Dynamics (PSID)			
1971	5.8	3.3	1.76
1977	6.8	3.8	1.79
1985	7.7	4.0	1.93

with U.S. Bureau of Labor Statistics injury and illness data by industry to estimate the percentage of black and white workers disabled on the job each year.

Rates of occupational injury and acute illness for black and white male workers are represented in table 28. For CPS men these rates increased from 5.7% among blacks and 3.2% among whites in 1968 to 6.5% among blacks and 4.6% among whites in 1986. The excess risk of injury and acute illness faced by black men as compared with white men declined, however, from 80% in 1968 to 40% in 1986. The PSID cohort also experienced an overall increase in injury rates, but the racial differential actually increased slightly.

Race-specific occupational injury rates for female workers are displayed in table 29. On-the-job injuries and acute illnesses became more prevalent for CPS women over this time period, growing from 2.3% for blacks and 1.4% for whites in 1968 to 4.5% for blacks and 2.3% for whites in 1986. The excess risk faced by black women as compared with their white coworkers declined from 60% in 1968 to 30% in 1977 but then

Table 29
*Percentage of Female Workers Suffering a Disabling
Occupational Injury or Acute Illness, 1968–1986*

	Black Workers	White Workers	B/W Ratio
Current Population Survey (CPS)			
1968	2.3	1.4	1.64
1977	3.0	2.3	1.30
1986	4.5	2.3	1.97
Panel Study of Income Dynamics (PSID)			
1971	3.8	2.5	1.52
1977	4.3	3.5	1.23
1985	4.3	2.3	1.87

jumped back up to 100% in 1986. A similar pattern is observed among women surveyed by the PSID, where the excess risk for blacks declined from 50% in 1971 to 20% in 1977 and then increased to 90% in 1985.

Comparison with Racial Differences in Unemployment and Earnings

It is instructive to compare racial differences in hazardous exposures with racial differences in unemployment and earnings. Unemployment rates for blacks and whites separately are available starting in 1972.[6] In that year, 4.5% of white men and 5.9% of white women were unemployed and looking for work. The comparable figures for black men and women were 10.4% and 11.8%. In 1986, unemployment rates for white men and women were 6.0% and 6.1%, while those for blacks were 14.5% and 14.2%. The excess risk of unemployment faced by blacks thus increased between 1972 and 1986 from 130% to 140% for men and from 100% to 130% for women.

Data on earnings by race are available starting in the 1940s and generally show a pattern of narrowing differentials. The validity of the wage data for recent years has been questioned, however, due to the decline in labor force participation among black as compared with white men. One would expect that those blacks leaving the labor force do so at least in part because they face relatively low wage rates, even compared with other blacks. If this is so, then the blacks who do remain in the labor force are the relatively skilled members of the black working population, and a comparison of their wages with those of all white workers would understate the true earnings disadvantage faced by blacks as a group relative to whites as a group. Relative earnings data that are corrected for the decline in labor force participation have been computed for the years between 1960 and 1978.[7] After correcting for differential changes in labor force participation, the racial gap in earnings has narrowed. The ratio of black to white earnings among male workers rose from 56% in 1960 to 61% in 1970 and thereafter remained stable. The relative progress of black women was much more impressive. They earned 63% as much as white women in 1960, 96% as much in 1970, and by 1978 earned the same as white women.

Conclusion

Hazardous jobs tend to be undesirable in terms of wages as well as working conditions, and they often are staffed by workers who have few alternative job options. These facts must be viewed in light of the earlier analyses of how workers perceive and respond to occupational safety and health hazards. As the statistical analyses in chapter 2 made clear, workers are aware of many of the health and safety hazards to which they are exposed, and respond to these perceptions in several ways. Quit rates tend to be higher in hazardous than in safe jobs, although the association is not always consistent. These inconsistencies suggest that workers are often aware of the hazards present in various jobs without having personally worked there, and so avoid the jobs altogether rather than sign on and then quit later. Workers also pursue collective strategies to improve working conditions. Representation elections are initiated and won by unions more frequently in industries with high injury rates than in industries with low injury rates.

Chapter 3 examined the direct effects of labor unions on working conditions through their collective bargaining and dispute arbitration systems. The indirect effects of unions on hazards may be even more important than the direct effects, because unions raise wages and improve fringe benefits at organized work sites.[8] These improved compensation packages make unionized jobs more attractive to skilled workers than they otherwise would have been. The tendency of unions to raise wages counteracts the tendency of management to reduce wages and skills in hazardous jobs. If some hazardous jobs require considerable skills and offer high wages despite labor market incentives to do the opposite, it is often precisely because of labor union initiatives. Historically, unions have raised wage levels in a number of important hazardous industries, including construction, mining, and lumber. Although hazardous, jobs in these industries have been attractive to white workers as well as to blacks. With the decline of unionization in these industries, relative wages are falling, and with them the attractiveness of risky jobs to workers who possess other options. Substitution of one labor force for another does not occur overnight, but it invariably follows significant changes in wages.

None of these observations contradict Adam Smith's theory of compensating differentials, as noted in chapter 5. After adjusting for skill requirements, hazardous jobs do pay more than safe jobs if the hazards are easily recognized by workers. But skill requirements differ across jobs and can be altered by management to reduce the need for workers who demand high hazard pay premiums. Indeed, the potential demand for hazard pay by skilled workers can be interpreted as the motor that drives the system toward reductions in skill requirements and wages and that fills hazardous occupations with disadvantaged workers.

This, then, is the logic of the labor market. Those workers with the most valuable skills and facing the least discrimination avoid hazardous jobs altogether or quit after learning about the risks. Collective worker and labor union efforts sometimes counter this tendency by raising wages and skill requirements in hazardous occupations, thereby making them attractive to a wider stratum of workers. Needless to say, employers do not accept this passively. Moves and countermoves on the shop floor generate industrial conflict, which in turn reduces productivity and profits. Weak profit rates and a depressed investment climate lead to a mood of economic uncertainty and concern for job security that chills shop floor worker initiatives.

Two crucial arenas for labor and management conflict have been neglected in the discussion so far: the legal and regulatory systems. The past thirty years have witnessed intense political conflict between employers and employees over occupational safety and health issues. This conflict has occurred at the national, state, and local levels and has become intertwined with broader debates over industrial relations, environmental quality, and public health. The next three chapters offer an analysis of these developments, focusing on how legal and regulatory strategies complement shop floor and labor market efforts to achieve better working conditions.

7

The Right to Know?

Fear of governmental authority and coercion has created a strong preference in liberal societies for market mechanisms to coordinate economic activity. The most important is the market for labor, which determines who shall work in which job for which wage and at what risk to health and safety. But authority and coercion are not limited to public institutions. Imbalances in power permeate private markets and in particular the labor market. Workers are especially vulnerable with respect to health hazards. Management has a strong advantage in generating and interpreting information on the health effects of workplace exposures to toxic substances and often can conceal this information from the work force. Management's right to hire and fire at will allows it to discriminate systematically against employees who educate themselves about the risks and are willing to provide leadership for their coworkers. One of the central problems of political philosophy in the modern era has been how to use governmental powers to limit force and fraud in private markets while maintaining the vitality of the markets themselves. As society's understanding of occupational health has grown, a similar debate has emerged over how to guarantee the worker's "right to know" about workplace hazards and "right to act" in response to that knowledge.

This chapter and the next analyze the movement to control deception and coercion in the labor market as a means for

achieving safer and healthier working conditions. This movement relies mainly on efforts outside the labor market, in the
legal and regulatory arenas, where the balance of power is different. In contrast to the exit and voice strategies discussed
earlier, which represent private efforts by individuals and organized groups, the emphasis now shifts to public efforts by
workers, labor unions, and their allies to achieve better working conditions. This chapter concentrates on the worker's
right to know, a political response to deception in the labor
market. The following chapter explores the worker's right to
act, an evolving response to coercion in the labor market.

A History of Fraud and Deception

Nothing has more characterized the history of occupational
health since the industrial revolution than the imbalance between employers and employees in access to hazard information. Many examples could be cited. The DBCP sterilization
case described in the Introduction resulted from the unwill-
ingness of the pesticide's manufacturer to follow up on clear
evidence in early studies of reproductive toxicity, which allowed workers to be exposed until health effects were widespread. The Union Carbide Corporation and its subcontrac-
tors concealed evidence of an epidemic of acute and often
fatal silicosis among tunnel workers in West Virginia.[1] The
Rohm and Haas Company ignored lung cancer among workers exposed to bischloromethylether (BCME), prevented independent analyses of exposure and medical records, and
sought to forestall governmental efforts to evaluate and regulate the substance.[2] The Allied-Signal chemical company was
sufficiently concerned about the neurotoxic effects of the pesticide kepone to create a legally separate corporate entity to
produce the substance; high exposures among uninformed
and unprotected workers caused serious tremors, brain damage, liver enlargement, personality changes, and sterility.[3]
Employers in mining industries refused to disclose to workers
the results of periodic chest X rays but instead used this infor-

mation to fire workers when their lung disease had progressed to a stage where they might consider filing a compensation claim.[4]

Two aspects of workplace deception stand out. Where the toxic substances are new and produced by only a few firms, industry has often denied the hazard existed and sought to prevent independent researchers from gaining access to data necessary to identify risks. Where the toxic substances are well known and widely used, industry has often concealed the extent of workplace exposures and medical evidence on adverse health effects in individual workers.

These tactics of obfuscation and deceit have been practiced most widely and effectively by the asbestos industry, which fought a decades-long battle to minimize the dangers of asbestosis, deny the association between asbestos and cancer, and conceal medical evidence of disease from individual employees. The asbestos story is particularly important because it proves how vulnerable workers are to fraud and deception in an unregulated labor market. In contrast to many of the examples cited above, asbestos was not a new hazard nor one produced by only a few firms. The dangers of asbestosis had been recognized since ancient times, when Roman slaves weaving asbestos textiles were given crude masks to reduce dust inhalation. By the 1930s, asbestos products were produced by dozens of firms and used in all industrialized nations. Numerous case reports of asbestosis and, later, cancer were published in the medical literature. Yet the U.S. asbestos industry was able to conceal the risks from most of their workers and minimize the costs of compensation and control until the 1970s.

The long cover-up of the asbestos epidemic has been extensively documented; a few examples of the *modus operandi* should suffice.[5] The asbestos industry restricted scientific understanding of the health risks through their control of access to the workplace. Outside researchers were only permitted access if they cooperated fully and agreed not to disclose the results of their studies to the workers. For example, the government's suggested exposure limit of five million particles per cubic foot (MPPCF) of air, which remained in place for decades, was established based upon a 1934 U.S. Public Health Service study of three North Carolina asbestos textile mills. Prior to inviting in the Public Health Service, the employers fired 150 out of a total of 600 workers based on their medical condition. As case reports spread regarding cancer among workers suffering from asbestosis, the industry argued that only a full-scale epidemiological study could prove any cancer link, but then systematically refused to allow researchers to study available data on employment and cancer incidence. This monopoly of information was broken by researchers using data from the British workers' compensation system and pension records from the U.S. asbestos insulators labor union.

Major asbestos producers maintained a policy of testing workers for lung problems but not informing them of the results. Labor union requests for access to these medical records were denied. Union quiescence was encouraged by the firms' policies of discharging workers who filed compensation claims and refusing to hire workers who quit or were fired from other asbestos firms and whose medical exams revealed adverse health effects. Johns-Manville, the largest asbestos firm, benefited from a very divided union movement; twenty-six different unions represented workers in the firm's various facilities during the 1960s. A six-month strike in 1971 at the firm's largest mill, in Manville, New Jersey, finally forced Johns-Manville to release the evidence on serious hazards produced by a confidential governmental study conducted in 1965.

The Right-to-Know Movement Begins

It is against this backdrop of management deception that the worker right-to-know movement was born in the 1970s. As discussed in the context of the DBCP case, the movement grew partly out of labor union efforts to improve working conditions. Given the many unorganized workplaces and the weakness of unions in many organized workplaces, the right-to-know movement quickly focused its efforts in the political arena. As early as 1974, the Philadelphia Area Project on Occupational Safety and Health (PHILAPOSH), a coalition of labor unions and community organizations, was pressing OSHA to promulgate a standard guaranteeing worker access to information on toxicity, exposures, and health effects. Development of a draft regulation began in earnest in 1977, with the inauguration of the Carter administration. OSHA initially coordinated efforts with the Environmental Protection Agency to produce a hazard labeling standard covering the general community as well as the workplace. This effort failed, and in 1980 OSHA decided to push ahead with a standard governing the labeling of hazardous substances encountered in the workplace. After President Carter was defeated in his reelection bid in November of 1980, OSHA rushed to complete its labeling regulation. The agency issued the Hazard Identification Standard just days before Ronald Reagan was inaugurated in January of 1981.[6]

The Hazard Identification Standard required manufacturers and importers of chemicals to assemble hazard evaluation files on each of their products and to inform their employees of any health risks. The regulation covered approximately 32,000 chemicals listed in the Registry of Toxic Effects of Chemical Substances, compiled by NIOSH. Employees of nonmanufacturing firms would be covered through the provisions requiring manufacturers and importers to supply purchasers of the chemicals with comprehensive labels. Labor unions would also have access to the hazard evaluation files and container labels. The labels would include the precise chemical identity of the contents. Precautionary statements about possible health effects and methods of handling would be included but would not be substituted for the chemical identity.

The Hazard Identification Standard would have required employers to inform their employees of the toxic effects generally known to be associated with substances used on the job, and thus would have dealt with the first type of deception in the labor market. It would not, however, have prevented employers from claiming that the actual exposures in their plants were safe. Given the history of employer refusals to release the results of exposure monitoring and medical tests, OSHA promulgated a separate standard in 1980 requiring employers to divulge such information to individual employees upon request. Labor union representatives and OSHA inspectors were guaranteed access to exposure records and to aggregations of medical data that maintained the confidentiality of the individual workers.

The Reagan Revolution Comes to OSHA

In one of its first acts of deregulation, the Reagan administration withdrew the Carter administration's Hazard Identification Standard on 12 February 1981. The revocation would "permit the Department [of Labor] to consider regulatory alternatives that had not been fully considered."[7] The form such an effort could take became apparent the next month when the Chemical Manufacturers Association (CMA) proposed an alternative approach to hazard communication.[8] The program would be voluntary, and thus no company could be disciplined by OSHA for failing to have an effective program.

The proposed CMA program differed from the Carter administration's regulation in a number of other ways. The CMA draft took a "performance," rather than a "specification," approach, allowing employers to decide which chemicals were hazardous and which were the most effective ways to warn employees about those hazards. In contrast to the Carter administration proposal, which required the inclusion of the chemical identity on container labels, the CMA proposal allowed employers to limit labels to precautionary statements and emergency treatments.

The CMA proposed to rely on the precautionary labeling guidelines developed by the industry-supported American

National Standards Institute (ANSI). The ANSI guidelines focused on acute health effects and downplayed the risks of chronic illness. Under the CMA plan, suspected adverse health effects would not be communicated to workers "until consensus definitions and test criteria for these chronic effects are established." With respect to chronic health effects such as cancer, behavioral alterations, and diminished mental awareness, the CMA proposal asserted that the current state of science and medicine was "insufficient to permit the development of definitions and criteria as standards to be used on a broad basis." The CMA followed up on its proposal by sponsoring an updating of the ANSI labeling guidelines. The revisions added new warnings for chronic health effects. The warnings were to be expressed "as simply and briefly as possible on labels affixed to containers of hazardous chemicals and in other written material. . . . The wording on precautionary labels [was not] expected to cover the complete information on the properties of a material."[9]

During its first year in office, the Reagan administration also tried to eviscerate OSHA's regulation guaranteeing worker and labor union access to company industrial hygiene and medical records. On 13 July 1982, OSHA proposed a number of revisions of the original regulation.[10] The revisions were designed to limit the chemicals and workers covered by the regulation, reduce the time during which records must be retained, and broaden the exemptions for trade secrets. The revisions dropped 90% of the substances originally covered by the standard. Employers would no longer have to retain records for workers employed less than one year, for construction workers, or for workers incidentally exposed to toxic substances when performing their regular work duties. Employers were granted broad rights to claim that chemical identities constituted trade secrets and hence to exclude them from coverage. Companies were required to identify chemicals known to cause cancer, birth defects, or other significant harm but only if there was a "need to know" the precise chemical name. Employers retained the authority to decide whether workers and their union representatives had this need for information. When employers did reveal trade secret information, the proposed revisions allowed them to require workers and union representatives to sign legally binding confidentiality agreements that provided for financial compensation to the employer in case the information leaked out. The original regulation on exposure and medical records expressly denied employers the right to require confidentiality agreements with compensation mechanisms.[11] The proposed modifications drew praise from industry groups such as the U.S. Chamber of Commerce, which had challenged the legality of the original regulation, and criticism from labor groups such as the AFL-CIO, which had considered the original exposure and medical records standard to be one of the most important of OSHA's regulations.[12]

The third major area in which the Reagan administration reversed the direction of OSHA's previous efforts to inform workers was the agency's own program of developing and disseminating educational materials. Under the Carter administration, OSHA had developed an ambitious program of sponsoring films, slide shows, pamphlets, posters, and other educational efforts designed to raise worker concern for occupational safety and health. These materials were distributed through labor unions, medical clinics, and other organizations. The program embodied a philosophy that educational efforts should not be exclusively under the control of employers. The guiding philosophy of OSHA under the Reagan administration was that management bore the responsibility for health and safety and therefore that the design of educational programs was management's prerogative.

On 27 March 1981, OSHA withdrew from circulation three films describing occupational hazards and the governmental regulatory process, slide shows on the hazards of acrylonitrile and cotton dust, and two brochures and a poster on cotton dust. The main reason for the withdrawal of these materials seemed to be the prominence given to photographs of workers and quotations by workers. The acrylonitrile slide show had drawn fire from the Society of the Plastics Industry (SPI). The SPI objected to the general tone of the show, which was accompanied by a proworker folk song that the SPI felt would have the effect of "stirring up discontent and uneasiness." The brochures and poster on cotton dust showed the face of a cotton mill worker accompanied by a caption stating that he had worked in the mills forty-four years and had died of brown lung disease. The agency had produced 100,000 copies of one brown lung brochure, 25,000 copies of the second, and 10,000 copies of the poster. All copies of these materials that had not already been distributed were destroyed. The two brochures were then reissued, minus the photograph and quotation from the mill worker.[13] The Reagan administration subsequently called a moratorium on production or procurement of educational materials until they could be evaluated. This moratorium covered slide shows that were being produced on lead, benzene, OSHA's cancer policy, access to medical records, and safety hazards.[14]

Organizing for the Right to Know

While the Reagan administration endeavored to roll back federal OSHA's involvement in worker education and training, a more diffuse, but ultimately more powerful, right-to-know movement was spreading across individual states and cities. The same labor, health, and environmental groups that had pushed for medical records access and hazard identification regulations in Washington also pursued similar policy strategies in their own neighborhoods. By the time Ronald Reagan was inaugurated, several right-to-know statutes were already being developed in union strongholds. The deregulatory strategy pursued by federal OSHA beginning in 1981 forced the occupational health activists to focus their attention on the state and local levels.

Philadelphia adopted one of the earliest and most effective local right-to-know regulations. The adoption of these rules, which took the form of amendments to the city's fire and air pollution codes, capped five years of organizing by the Philadelphia Area Project on Occupational Safety and Health. PHILAPOSH was founded by activists from the Oil, Chemical, and Atomic Workers International Union employed in the many oil refineries in the area.[15] It grew rapidly and by 1980 included over seventy local union sponsors ranging from industrial workers to teachers, welfare workers, and caretakers in the Philadelphia zoo. PHILAPOSH's main focus of activity was to provide workers and labor unions with technical information and training in health and safety issues. The group lobbied federal OSHA for a hazard communication standard and then decided to pursue one in Philadelphia. It helped establish the Delaware Valley Toxics Coalition, an alliance of labor, community, and environmental groups, and mounted a political campaign to overcome the resistance of the Philadelphia business community. The coalition packed city council meetings with hundreds of supporters and linked worker right-to-know issues with citizen concerns for environmental health in Philadelphia's industrial neighborhoods. This was one of the first explicit linkages between access to information on hazards in the workplace and access to information on hazards in the surrounding community. The city council ultimately adopted a compromise version of the amendments on 22 January 1981. Ironically, this was the same week that Reagan's OSHA withdrew the Carter administration's Hazard Identification Standard.

The next several years saw the adoption of a wide variety of laws, regulations, and ordinances across the nation that required firms to disclose the identity of the hazardous substances they used. By the end of 1983, fifteen states and dozens of communities had disclosure laws; twenty more states and uncounted communities were actively considering such legislation.[16] The details of these laws, regulations, and ordinances differed substantially. Some were restricted to particular sectors of industry, while others covered all workplaces and extended to the community at large. Different statutes covered different chemicals. Protections for trade secrets were broad in some jurisdictions but narrow in others. These state and local right-to-know statutes were sponsored by activists from labor unions, community groups, environmental organizations, and coalitions such as PHILAPOSH. The statutes then served to encourage further activism.

A law passed in New York in 1980 played a pivotal role in worker and labor union health and safety activities in that state over the next several years.[17] The worker activities encouraged by the New York right-to-know law spanned the breadth of the state's industries and occupations. A tool manufacturer near Syracuse was cited for refusing to provide information on toxic substances to a former employee suffering from a hard metals disease.[18] A plastics manufacturer near Rochester agreed to train its employees about hazard exposures and take other steps to comply with the state law after being cited for excessive delay in responding to requests for hazard information by the labor union representing its employees.[19] Three labor unions filed charges with the attorney general's office against the State University of New York in Oswego after employees were instructed to remove some asbestos insulation and were told that it was merely mineral wool.[20] An international accounting firm with offices in several parts of the state agreed to train employees in its graphic arts, printing, and word-processing departments concerning proper handling methods for hexane, trichloroethane, and methylene chloride.[21] In New York City, American Telephone and Telegraph agreed to pay a large fine and train 8,000 employees concerning the toxicity and safe handling procedures for polychlorinated biphenyls (PCBs), mercury vapor tubes, lead cell batteries, asbestos, freon, adhesives, lead, and methylene chloride.[22] A small resin optics company in Elmira was cited for firing a worker who requested hazard information and a transfer to a safer job after becoming pregnant. The discharge violated the right to refuse hazardous work clause in the state law.[23] Under the provisions of two state environmental protection acts, as well as the worker right-to-know act, a wholesale greenhouse company near Rochester was cited for failing to inform fifty workers concerning the hazards of pesticides, for poisoning nearby wetlands, and for failing to fence off pesticide-contaminated areas to prevent children from playing there.[24]

OSHA's Hazard Communication Standard

The proliferation of right-to-know laws and ordinances at the political grass roots prompted federal OSHA to consider a national hazard communication regulation of its own, less than a year after it had withdrawn Carter's standard. This turnabout was engineered by the Chemical Manufacturers Association and several large chemical firms that were becoming concerned with the costs of complying with different labeling standards in different parts of the country. They abandoned the notion of a voluntary policy and pushed OSHA to promulgate a mandatory standard. In the process they found themselves in the novel position of fighting to overcome the deregulatory philosophy of the White House.[25]

The key feature of the CMA proposal was the principle that a federal standard could preempt more stringent state and local standards. This signified a completely new relationship between federal OSHA and the various state health and safety programs. Under the 1970 Occupational Safety and Health Act, states were allowed to develop their own laws and agencies, provided these were "at least as effective as" the federal law and agency.[26] Federal regulations thus served as a floor below which states were not allowed to fall. Now, federal OSHA would pass a regulation to serve as a ceiling above which no state was allowed to climb.

In March 1982, OSHA published a proposed Hazard Communication Standard. Opposition from within various parts of the Reagan administration delayed its promulgation for another year and a half, and it was not until November 1983 that the standard was issued.[27] The rule required that manufacturers and importers of chemicals provide their industrial customers with labeled containers and Material Safety Data Sheets (MSDS) containing additional information on toxicity. Firms in the manufacturing sector were required to distribute these to their customers and employees. Manufacturers also were required to develop a hazard education and training program including, but not limited to, the dissemination of the labels and data sheets. Firms were given wide latitude regarding the form of the education and training programs. Firms outside the manufacturing sector were not required to develop such programs.

The Hazard Communication Standard raised a storm of criticism from labor and environmental groups involved in the right-to-know movement. The restriction of the standard to the manufacturing sector, which eliminated two-thirds of the nation's workers from coverage, was criticized as arbitrary. OSHA had justified the restriction as consistent with a policy of targeting the most hazardous sectors of the economy. While many of the most hazardous exposures do occur among manufacturing workers, there are significant exposures at many nonmanufacturing work sites. Opponents pointed to data from the U.S. Bureau of Labor Statistics indicating that nine nonmanufacturing industries experienced rates of chemical-related injuries and illnesses higher than those experienced by the majority of manufacturing industries.[28] A national exposure survey conducted in 1972 and 1973 by the National Institute for Occupational Safety and Health found hospital workers to be potentially exposed to thirty-eight chemical products per facility, compared with twenty-three chemical products per facility for manufacturing workers. OSHA's restriction of the Hazard Communication Standard to manufacturing was even criticized by other wings of the Reagan administration. The National Institute for Occupational Safety and Health pointed out the high level of hazardous exposures in construction, maintenance work, auto repair, and other industries. The Department of Defense was concerned for federal employees working in environments similar to those in the private sector but excluded from any right to know about hazardous substances.[29]

Another feature of the new Hazard Communication Standard that raised the ire of critics was the manner in which individual substances were to be classified. Consistent with its philosophy that firms should be given freedom in deciding how to implement the standard, OSHA assigned to employers the responsibility for deciding which substances were hazardous and which were not. The agency did indicate that a set of 416 chemicals known to pose cancer risks had to be included in an employer's program if the chemicals were used by that employer.[30] The process of determining whether a particular substance poses risks to human health is a complex one, made difficult by gaps in scientific knowledge and by the inherent necessity of making value-laden judgments in cases where the evidence is ambiguous. Critics of the OSHA rule feared that reliance on employer judgment would result in what NIOSH predicted would be "poor, erroneous, and conflicting" hazard determinations at different work sites.[31] They preferred an alternative approach whereby OSHA would take responsibility for hazard determination and provide employers with the list of substances that must be covered. Substances not on OSHA's list would not have to be evaluated by employers.[32]

The Hazard Communication Standard also allowed employers to withhold information that would reveal specific chemical identities if the employers felt those identities were trade secrets of interest to competitors. Access to proprietary information of this sort would be permitted for physicians and other health professionals if they could demonstrate a "need to know." In nonemergency situations, health professionals could be made to sign confidentiality agreements that included provisions for financial compensation if the trade secret information leaked out. Critics saw ample opportunity for abuse of the notion of trade secrets in order to prevent, or at least delay, disclosure of information on hazards.

The Hazard Communication Standard in Court

On 22 November 1983, the United Steelworkers Union of America and Ralph Nader's Public Citizen organization sued OSHA over its new Hazard Communication Standard. The AFL-CIO and a number of states that already had right-to-know laws and feared preemption by the federal rule joined the petitioners. They argued that the restriction of the standard to manufacturing was arbitrary, that OSHA, rather than employers, should bear the responsibility for deciding which chemicals are hazardous, and that the trade secrets exemptions were too broad.[33] On 24 May 1985, the Third Circuit Court of Appeals upheld some parts of the standard and rejected others. The court found the restriction of the Hazard Communication Standard to manufacturing to be unjustified, and required OSHA to extend it to the rest of industry. The trade secrets exemptions were found to be too inclusive. The court upheld, however, the delegation to industry of the primary responsibility for deciding which substances should be considered hazardous.[34]

Although ordered by the court to issue a revised Hazard Communication Standard that would cover nonmanufacturing industries and restrict the trade secrets exemptions, OSHA delayed action for another year and a half. The agency was again sued by the United Steelworkers and Public Citizen, who claimed that "a more extreme case of unreasonable delay would be difficult to imagine."[35] On 29 May 1987, the court ruled that within sixty days OSHA had to issue a Hazard Communication Standard covering nonmanufacturing industries. OSHA sought a stay of the order so as to have time to appeal the decision to the Supreme Court but abandoned the effort when the Justice Department withdrew its support.[36] On 24 August 1987, OSHA finally promulgated an expanded rule as required by the court.[37]

The promulgation of the expanded Hazard Communication Standard did not signal an end to the Reagan administration's resistance to a comprehensive right-to-know policy, but rather a shift in the locus of opposition from OSHA itself to the Office of Management and Budget (OMB). The OMB is an entity in the executive branch of the government whose mandate is to oversee the activities of the various regulatory agencies, including OSHA.[38] OMB is well known for its hostility to regulation in general and occupational health regulation in particular. Armed with various statutes and executive orders from the president, the OMB reviews, delays, and often rescinds regulatory initiatives coming from OSHA. It responded to the expanded Hazard Communication Standard in customary style.

While narrow in the specifics of its objections, the OMB opposition led OSHA to reopen completely the Hazard Communication Standard for public comments and possible amendment.[39] Faced with the prospect of having to start a new, lengthy rule-making process, supporters of the Hazard Communication Standard counterattacked. The United Steelworkers and Public Citizen petitioned the Third Circuit Court of Appeals to make the standard enforceable as originally envisaged and to prohibit OSHA and the OMB from creating any further legal impediments.[40] Representatives of the construction industry, who were particularly opposed to the extension of the standard beyond the manufacturing sector, then took their case to the U.S. Supreme Court.[41] The federal Department of Justice intervened in the case on the side of the construction industry, arguing that OMB's ability to control regulatory activities was at stake.[42]

In a legal decision with potentially far-reaching implications for regulatory policy as a whole, the Supreme Court on 21 February 1990 upheld the Hazard Communication Standard.[43] The construction industry had won almost a year of delay in the enforcement of the right-to-know standard, but at a high price. The Supreme Court ruled that the OMB's authority was limited to regulations that required businesses to submit information to the government itself. Regulations requiring the disclosure of information to other parties, such as employees, were not subject to control by the OMB. This interpretation would limit OMB's ability to rescind other forms of disclosure requirements, such as food labeling at the Food and Drug Administration and the environmental pollution warning requirements at the Environmental Protection Agency.

Preemption of State Right-to-Know Laws: OSHA's Pyrrhic Victory

The Reagan administration's effort to forestall the passage of new state and local standards faced two contradictory impulses. On the one hand, their philosophical hostility toward governmental regulation predisposed OSHA, the Office of Management and Budget, and other parts of the administration toward narrow, restricted regulations. On the other hand, in order for OSHA's standard to preempt its state and local competitors successfully, it needed to be broad and strong enough to convince the courts that it would do an effective job. The key features of the Hazard Communication Standard as originally promulgated—its restriction to manufacturing, its limited list of substances covered, its broad protection of trade secrets, and its exclusion of environmental emissions— turned out to be its Achilles' heel. While the basic principle that the federal government could preempt state and local laws won in court, this turned out to be a Pyrrhic victory for OSHA. The courts held that the narrow OSHA standard could only partially and not completely preempt broader state standards. The undermining of the original preemption purpose of the OSHA standard was fought out in two battles concerning the New Jersey and Pennsylvania right-to-know laws.

The New Jersey Worker and Community Right to Know Act was signed into law by the governor of that state on 23 August 1983. It covered all industries, not just manufacturing, and also governed emissions of toxic substances into the general environment.[44] The law required employers to file with the state a completed survey for every toxic substance used, including the chemical name, a description of its uses, the quantitites used and transported, and methods of storage and transport. In addition, firms had to report all emissions into the general environment from smokestacks and other intended sources as well as unintended emissions such as spills. Employers had to file a list of workplace hazardous substances with various state agencies, the county health department, and local police and fire departments. The state agencies were to make this information available to citizens upon request.

On 10 October 1985, the U.S. District Court for New Jersey ruled that the New Jersey law was preempted by the federal Hazard Communication Standard for the manufacturing sector.[45] Nonmanufacturing employers were still required to comply, since the federal standard did not cover nonmanufacturing industries at that time. This ruling was considered a major victory for the Reagan administration but already made clear that OSHA's Hazard Communication Standard would have to be extended to nonmanufacturing industries in order to fulfill its purpose of preempting state and local initiatives. The scope of the preemption was narrowed, however, in a subsequent review of the case by the Third Circuit Court of Appeals. In a partial reversal of the lower court's order, the court of appeals ruled that manufacturing employers in New Jersey had to comply with those portions of the state law that concerned environmental emissions and access to information by community members, since the federal standard did not cover these matters.[46]

The Pennsylvania right-to-know statute, signed into law on 5 October 1984, followed the New Jersey model in many respects.[47] It required the state Department of Labor and Industry to compile a list of hazardous substances, based on lists developed by various scientific and governmental bodies, and forward it to each of the state's 26,000 employers. Every manufacturer, importer, and supplier would thereafter be required to include a Material Safety Data Sheet with every shipment of any chemical on the list. These sheets were required to list the exact chemical name and all relevant information on toxicity, handling procedures, and proper disposal methods. Employers were also required to fill out surveys covering the quantities of each of the hazardous substances used in the past year. Copies of these surveys were to be posted in the workplace, forwarded to the state agency, and provided to local fire, police, and emergency response personnel upon request.

The Pennsylvania right-to-know statute was quickly contested in court in a lawsuit brought by a group of manufacturing companies. On 12 December 1985, a U.S. district court ruled that the Pennsylvania law was preempted for the manufacturing sector but not for nonmanufacturing industries.[48] In a subsequent decision, however, the Third Circuit Court of Appeals decided that the Pennsylvania law was not completely preempted, even in the manufacturing sector, since it was stronger in many ways than the federal law.[49] In particular, the court ruled that manufacturing, as well as nonmanufacturing, firms in Pennsylvania would have to report data on the quantities of hazardous substances used each year, treat as hazardous those materials not on OSHA's list but included in the state of Pennsylvania's broader list, and comply with the requirements to supply local fire, police, and emergency response personnel with data upon request. In essence, the court ruled that OSHA's standard preempted only those aspects of the state law that were equivalent to the federal standard. Those parts of the state law that went beyond the federal standard were not preempted.

The ruling on the Pennsylvania law was immediately recognized as far-reaching. It implied the defeat of OSHA's basic strategy of promulgating restricted federal standards and then using these to strike down more extensive state and local statutes. Industry groups had responded to the earlier preemption of the New Jersey state law for the manufacturing sector through a strategy focused on extending the federal standard to cover nonmanufacturing industries. The Pennsylvania ruling undermined this strategy, since it meant that the mere existence of a federal standard covering nonmanufacturing industries would not prevent states and localities from promulgating rules and regulations more stringent than the federal one.[50]

The Community's Right to Know

The initial impetus for guarantees of worker and citizen access to information on hazardous substances came from labor unions and other worker-oriented groups. Faced with management resistance to occupational health initiatives both on the shop floor and at OSHA, workers and labor unions sought a new set of political allies. Shop floor activism was hit hard by the major economic recession of 1981 and 1982, the rise of competition from imported goods, and the growth of management resistance to collective bargaining. The environmental movement, in contrast, grew during the 1980s, in part propelled by growing citizen concern about the release of toxic substances into the air and into public drinking water.

Of decisive importance for the right-to-know movement was the chemical disaster in Bhopal, India, in December 1984.[51] An accidental release of methyl isocyanate from a Union Carbide pesticide-manufacturing plant killed an estimated 2,000 Bhopal residents and injured tens of thousands more. Although chemical industry representatives insisted that a comparable disaster could not happen in the United States, a major pesticide release later occurred at a Union Carbide plant in West Virginia. Much less serious than the Bhopal catastrophe, the methyl isocyanate leak from the West Virginia plant nevertheless led 130 persons to seek emergency treatment.

Following the response pattern pioneered by OSHA, the Environmental Protection Agency unveiled a voluntary chemical emergency program modeled after a plan developed by the Chemical Manufacturers Association. This plan would not have required employers to participate and would have allowed participating employers to exclude from the program any substance they considered to be a trade secret. Congress was not impressed by EPA's proposal and began drafting legislation that would impose stringent requirements on all major producers and users of toxic substances. Formally included as part of the legislation reauthorizing the federal hazardous waste cleanup program, commonly known as Superfund, the Emergency Planning and Community Right to Know Act (EPCRA) was a major legislative initiative in its own right. Modeled explicitly on OSHA's Hazard Communication Standard, the new legislation extended right-to-know provisions from the workplace to the general community.[52] EPCRA pursued the right-to-know logic substantially beyond the provisions of the OSHA standard, imposing new recordkeeping and disclosure obligations on firms and authorizing the establishment of state and community structures to use the newly available information.[53]

While the EPCRA legislation is complex and touches on many issues, its core is composed of three distinct programs. The first is an extension of the Hazard Communication Standard from the workplace to the community. Companies must provide various state and local authorities an annual inventory of toxic chemicals used or stored at each plant. All toxic substances incorporated in the OSHA standard are covered by this provision, and the OSHA-mandated Material Safety Data Sheets must accompany the chemical inventories. Second, major facilities that use toxic chemicals must keep records of their routine emissions and submit this information annually to EPA and the states. These data will hopefully provide estimates of trends in the magnitude and composition of toxic releases into the environment.

EPCRA's third and potentially most innovative component seeks to establish the institutional capacity to respond to new information on toxic chemical inventories and emissions. The greatest weakness in the workplace right-to-know strategy is the low level of union organization in U.S. industry and the paucity of other mechanisms to ensure that hazard information is understood and used. EPCRA requires the creation of state and local planning committees that will organize responses to emergency toxic releases and to the chemical inventory and emissions data. Firms are required to collaborate with the state and local committees if they have on-site a significant quantity of any chemical defined by EPA as "extremely hazardous."

Conclusion

The political evolution of the right-to-know movement over the course of the 1980s was remarkable. After a fragile beginning during the Carter presidency, the movement suffered a severe and almost fatal series of setbacks at the hands of the incoming Reagan administration. Few would have guessed that a mere five years later OSHA would promulgate a Hazard Communication Standard covering nonmanufacturing and manufacturing industries, that broad new rights to information would be guaranteed to communities through the federal hazardous waste legislation, and that toxics populism would be sweeping through the states. The right-to-know movement succeeded in linking workplace health risks with community health risks in the eyes of the citizenry and thereby built political coalitions throughout the nation. Although it won several battles, the Reagan administration seemed to lose the war. Unable to seize the initiative, it was forced to adopt and then abandon a series of defensive positions as the right-to-know movement gained momentum.

Over the course of the 1980s, workers and labor unions achieved more success in the political arena than they did in the economic arena, largely owing to their ability to link up with environmental organizations. This proved the importance of developing public strategies directed at the legislatures and judiciary as an alternative to more private strategies such as collective bargaining. The ultimate effectiveness of the various right-to-know laws and regulations in reducing occupational illness will depend, however, on shop floor mechanisms for interpreting the scientific data and coordinating worker responses. The natural institution to perform this role is the labor union. Unions, however, have been going through a period of severe contraction. Yet while collective bargaining has declined, labor law has undergone important changes that open up possibilities for new worker initiatives. The politics of occupational health have moved beyond the right to know toward the right to act.

8

The Right to Act?

The past thirty years have witnessed a dramatic development of laws, regulations, and collective bargaining agreements guaranteeing worker and community access to information on toxic substances. Access to information, however, is only one of four basic workers' rights, forming one component of an adequate system of worker representation.[1] The other components are due process (the fair and impartial adjudication of differences between employees and employers), free speech (the right to voice opinions without reprisal from management), and the right of association (the ability to join with others pursuing common goals). Together, these constitute the minimum necessary protections against employer force and fraud. They are the labor market analogue of the civil rights guaranteed to citizens in a political democracy. As the information-oriented right-to-know agenda is gradually put in place, there is, as one would expect, growing interest in developing the other three components of a grass-roots strategy for controlling occupational hazards. Activism is shifting from the right to know to the right to act.

At first glance, the interest in the right to act may seem strange. After all, the four workers' rights are already guaranteed under U.S. labor law. As embodied in the National Labor Relations Act, the rulings of the National Labor Relations Board, and various court interpretations, U.S. law supports workers' rights by supporting labor union rights. The right of association has been the cornerstone of industrial relations policy in the United States since 1935, when workers were guaranteed the right to join labor unions and employers were required to bargain in good faith with those unions over wages and working conditions. The law explicitly bans employers' attempts to limit the free speech rights of workers insofar as these relate to organizing unions and pursuing union strategies. Virtually all contracts negotiated by unions establish grievance and arbitration mechanisms that guarantee due process and fairness in the adjudication of individual claims. Finally, as discussed in chapter 3, the NLRB has consistently interpreted the employer's duty to bargain in good faith as implying a legally enforceable duty to provide unions with information concerning working conditions.

If the right to act is such a controversial issue, it must be because the collective bargaining system established by the NLRA is no longer capable of fulfilling its mandated function. Indeed, the system is in a state of dire crisis, and its survival without radical alteration is quite doubtful. The rapid decline in the fraction of the private sector work force that is represented by labor unions, documented in chapter 2, is only the most obvious symptom of a fundamental process of change. Equally, if not more, important are two other developments, which have contributed to the decline of collective bargaining and have helped satisfy worker needs that the collective bargaining system was never well designed to handle.

The first of the two novel developments has been the rise of the human resources management movement, a nonunion and often explicitly antiunion effort to reorganize industrial relations in order to promote worker satisfaction and productivity without the adversarial relations that traditionally accompany collective bargaining. Building upon research and experimentation in new and largely nonunion plants in the 1950s and 1960s, this managerialist approach offers many features pioneered by unionized industrial relations systems. In particular, it promotes a team or group approach to production, adjudication of discipline cases by an independent personnel department, an atmosphere of trust and free flow of information between workers and management, and some recognition of employees' rights to criticize the employer's policies at work and in the public domain. In short, the human resources movement partially guarantees each of the four essential workers' rights, but in a system that excludes independent, worker-controlled organizations.

The second development in industrial relations has come from government and provides striking evidence of the citizenry's declining faith in unionism as the solution to problems in the employment relationship. Whereas the NLRA guaranteed one basic right to workers—the right to join unions—the trend in industrial relations law over the past thirty years has been to enact statutes that provide specific rights on specific issues to specific groups of workers. The most dramatic of these, the Civil Rights Act of 1964, has dealt with employment discrimination, but other statutes have covered a plethora of other topics. Lacking a central focus or guiding principle, these new laws have offered a patchwork of rights to individual workers, particularly in the areas of due process, free speech, and access to information. They have been weakest in the area of the right of association. Nevertheless, these new public initiatives challenge unionism and private collective bargaining as the sole source of workers' rights. They embody an alternative strategy for controlling workplace hazards.

This strategy is individualistic in orientation, since it largely emphasizes the rights of particular individuals rather than of workers as a group. It is public rather than private, since it relies on the judicial system and administrative agencies rather than worker mobility in the labor market to achieve its ends.

This chapter analyzes the debate over the worker's right to act on health and safety issues within the context of these fundamental changes in industrial relations. It begins with the collective bargaining system, describing the weaknesses responsible for the success of the nonunion alternative. The features of the private sector managerialist strategy and of the public sector guarantees of employee rights are then considered in terms of what they offer to workers and community residents concerned with health risks.

Crisis in the System of Union Representation

Chapters 2 and 3 document a basic irony in society's efforts to control occupational safety and health hazards. Labor unions, which in American labor law and policy are to be the main representatives of worker interests, have significantly improved the breadth and depth of their health and safety activities over the past three decades. During precisely the same period, however, the percentage of the private sector work force represented by labor unions has dropped precipitously. Despite the strong and consistent association between hazardous exposures and worker desire for union representation, the decline in unionization has occurred most rapidly in the most hazardous industries. This erosion of union strength has been partly caused by management's increased use of illegal tactics to maintain a "union-free" environment. Employer animosity to unionism is not new, however, and the spread in antiunion campaigning must be interpreted as a symptom of deeper ills in the collective bargaining system. Now over fifty years old, the industrial relations framework established during the New Deal is proving incapable of responding adequately to changing public perceptions of the appropriate methods for resolving workplace conflicts.[2]

The National Labor Relations Act of 1935 constituted a historic compromise that guaranteed important rights to union organizations in exchange for the promise of stability and a containment of open conflict. The new industrial unions that emerged in the 1930s and 1940s adapted themselves to an authoritarian organization of production that was already firmly in place. To guarantee job security and limit favoritism, they negotiated for rules that governed promotion, grievance, and layoff procedures. To balance the otherwise overwhelming labor market power of corporate employers, they pioneered firmwide and industrywide collective bargaining concerning wages and conditions of employment. Unions sought exclusive representation for production workers in each workplace where they enjoyed majority support. Workers in firms where only a minority of employees supported the union gained no representation at all. After an initial turbulent period, unions developed into bureaucratic organizations that mirrored the bureaucratic corporations with which they were paired.

The collective bargaining framework offers a particular interpretation of the four fundamental workers' rights. The cornerstone of the system is the right of association within a labor union that serves as the exclusive representative of the work force. Second, unions have successfully bargained for grievance and arbitration mechanisms that guarantee due process and fairness in limiting management's ability to discipline workers without just cause. Under the "employment-at-will" doctrine fashioned by the courts during the nineteenth century, employers had the right to discipline or discharge an employee for any reason, including reasons completely unrelated to performance on the job.[3] The union grievance and arbitration mechanisms have effectively replaced this "at-will" policy with a "just cause" system.[4] Third, the National Labor Relations Board has interpreted the NLRA as granting significant protection for worker freedom of speech insofar as this relates to organizing a union or pursuing a union strategy at organized work sites. Fourth, the employer's duty to bargain in good faith has been interpreted as requiring management to provide the union with information on workplace hazards and other issues.[5]

While Byzantine in the intricacies of its implementation, the system of exclusive representation and collective bargaining provides a conceptually simple method for guaranteeing workers' rights. Given the imbalance of labor market power, labor unions are established as a countervailing force representing the interests of the work force. Rights are not assigned to individual workers directly but rather indirectly, through the assignation of rights to labor unions. Employers are obligated to bargain in good faith with unions, but not to treat individual workers with good faith. Due process and fairness are guaranteed through the grievance and arbitration mechanism, but it is the union rather than the individual worker that has the authority to decide which grievances to pursue and which to abandon. Employers must provide relevant information to the union, but individual workers do not possess any right to know. Unions are granted the right to strike, but individual workers enjoy only the weakest of protections when refusing to perform hazardous tasks.

The decline of the collective bargaining system can ultimately be traced to two assumptions that were valid fifty years ago but are no longer valid today. First, the balance-of-power principle embodied in the NLRA assumes that independent organizations are necessary to protect workers' rights and that individual workers will choose to be represented by these organizations. In retrospect, the failure of paternalistic employer policies to maintain employee loyalty during the period leading up to the 1935 legislation was an aberration caused by economic crisis and failure of vision. Since that time, the creative initiative in industrial relations has shifted decisively from unions to employers, who have developed new ways to provide some of the benefits of union representation in a nonunion environment.

The second assumption underlying the NLRA was that individual employees would acquiesce in the public delegation of rights to union organizations rather than directly to workers. The growing public distrust of large organizations and institutions has undermined this assumption and has led to an explosion of legislation that vests particular workers with particular rights. At the same time that the original balance of power between management and unions was being tipped decisively in management's direction, a new locus of worker power emerged in the federal and state judiciary.

The Nonunion Alternative

The most direct challenge to the collective bargaining system has come from the nonunion human resources management movement, which has developed in response to changes in the structure of production and employment over the past fifty years.[6] Abandoning the balance-of-power principle, this movement emphasizes the common interests joining employers and employees. The new managerialist philosophy supports worker voice mechanisms as a source of job satisfaction and enhanced productivity. Combining a team approach to production with formal dispute resolution mechanisms, this industrial relations system has defeated numerous union organizing efforts and prevented countless others.

The managerialist strategy has evolved out of several decades of experimentation with industrial relations policies based on new theories of worker motivation, satisfaction, and productivity. In direct contrast to the earlier assumption that workers will shirk their jobs if not kept under tight supervision and discipline, the new framework assumes that workers seek variety, challenge, autonomy, and the opportunity to learn new skills on the job. Rather than break work tasks into ever smaller components in an ever finer division of labor, the new approach organizes individual work tasks into processes that can be assigned to groups of workers who function as semiautonomous teams. In lieu of the earlier insistence upon command, the model now is coordination.

Supporting the new focus on motivation and team effort, the managerialist strategy provides a system that partially protects the rights of individual workers. Most importantly, personnel offices have been authorized to review discipline cases and function as impartial arbitrators between workers and supervisors.[7] In many cases these dispute resolution mechanisms are patterned explicitly upon grievance and arbitration mechanisms established under collective bargaining, albeit with less emphasis upon outside arbitration as the final step in the process. Breaking with the adversarial philosophy embodied in earlier industrial relations systems, the managerialist approach also emphasizes a free flow of information between workers and managers and an atmosphere more open to discussion, debate, and criticism. This greater freedom of expression is useful both as a means for obtaining new ideas from workers concerning improvements in the production process and as a means for developing worker commitment to the goals of the firm.

The work teams, "quality of work life" programs, ombudsman mechanisms, suggestion boxes, employee opinion surveys, and other innovations combine to make managerialist systems more open to worker participation and voice than many unionized systems. Unions have understandably reacted to these innovations with skepticism, because their explicit purpose is often to reduce employee interest in union representation. Analyses of a large 1983 survey of human resources policies and union representation elections in manufacturing firms confirm the effectiveness of these programs in thwarting unions. Approximately three-fourths of the firms surveyed had formal grievance systems and employee participation programs for their nonunion employees. Firms that developed these innovations in their new plants were significantly more successful in preventing the occurrence of union representation elections and in winning those elections that did occur than were firms without these mechanisms.[8]

The new nonunion industrial relations policies threaten the viability of labor unionism and collective bargaining in the core of the economy. Analyses of union representation elections find that union success rates are significantly higher in small firms than in big ones, a dramatic reversal of earlier patterns.[9] To maintain membership support, unions are often forced to struggle against the new worker participation programs and insist on strict separation between labor and management. Born partly out of worker resentment against the dehumanizing effects of the division of labor, unions ironically find themselves fighting to maintain that division and prevent any blurring of the line between production and managerial functions.[10]

Individual workers recognize the union emphasis on separation of managerial and production tasks. Substantially more nonunion workers interviewed in 1984 felt job characteristics such as wages, fringe benefits, and health and safety

conditions would improve after unionization than felt opportunities for worker participation would improve.[11] In a series
of five case studies, strong majorities of union members
rated highly the success of their representatives in improving wages, fringe benefits, and protection against unfair
treatment but did not rate their unions highly in terms of
improving productivity or representing worker interests in
management decision making.[12]

Rights for Individual Workers

In marked contrast to their success in preventing unionization, human resource management policies have been ineffective in slowing the growth of governmental interventions in
the workplace. Governmental policy of the New Deal era established unions as the exclusive representatives of employees
and then generally stood back and acquiesced in the outcomes of the bargaining process. Beginning most dramatically with the Civil Rights Act of 1964, government has enacted an evergrowing set of restrictions on management
prerogatives, thereby supplanting many of the functions traditionally assigned to labor unions. These restrictions have
been established in response to a strong current of public
opinion that distrusts both unions and management and in-
sists upon public guarantees of individual worker rights.

The single most important governmental incursion into
management authority has been in the domain of hiring and
firing, which began with state and federal civil rights legislation and has more recently included laws banning discrimination against individuals based upon age, handicap,
pregnancy, sexual orientation, political activity, or mari-
tal status.[13] These statutes have seriously eroded the
employment-at-will doctrine. According to this doctrine, employers and employees form a relationship for mutually beneficial reasons, and either side can terminate the relationship
when it ceases to be beneficial. Employees can quit at any

time for any reason. By analogy, in the words of the Tennessee State Supreme Court in 1884, employers "may dismiss their employees at-will . . . for good cause, for no cause, or even for cause morally wrong, without thereby being guilty of a legal wrong."[14]

The earliest breach in the employment-at-will doctrine was made by the NLRA of 1935, which prohibited discharges of workers supporting unionization. Civil rights legislation pioneered by several states and adopted by the federal government in 1964 effectively eliminated at-will discharges for minority workers. Under the federal statute, an employer is required to demonstrate that a discharge is due to unacceptable work performance as part of its burden of proving that the discharge is not due to racial prejudice. There exist similar limitations on the at-will doctrine for older workers, handicapped workers, and others protected by antidiscrimination statutes. Public employees are often covered by civil service systems that require proof of malfeasance prior to discipline.

Another major incursion into the employment-at-will doctrine has been made by the courts, which have increasingly reversed discharges where workers are disciplined for acts benefiting the larger public. This "public policy exception" applies to discharges of workers who refuse to carry out illegal acts for their employers (such as providing false testimony to a court), who perform an important public function (such as alerting the authorities to an employer's criminal behavior), or who exercise a statutory right (such as filing a Workers' Compensation claim after an occupational injury).[15] The protection against discharge for "whistle-blower" employees who alert governmental authorities to acts of employer crime has also been included in numerous statutes, including the Occupational Safety and Health Act, the Clean Air Act, and the Federal Water Pollution Control Act.[16] These provisions make it an offense for an employee to be fired or otherwise discriminated against for activities that promote the achievement of the specific goals of the statute.[17] Courts may not only force employers to compensate employees for economic losses incurred, but may also impose punitive damages for flagrant violations. Such lawsuits may emerge as an effective strategy for workers in a era without strong union organizations.[18]

Governmental bodies have promulgated a growing number of statutes and regulations that force corporations to divulge information to employees, consumers, and the general citizenry. Earliest among these were requirements for the labeling of foods and drugs and disclosures of information to stockholders, creditors, and borrowers. Chapter 7 discussed the important extension of disclosure principles to cover occupational exposures and environmental emissions of toxic substances.

Despite the proliferation of these statutes, the public protection of workers' rights is uneven and incomplete. None of the four fundamental workers' rights is firmly established. The vast majority of private sector workers are still subject to discipline and discharge under the employment-at-will doctrine. Workers refusing to perform hazardous jobs who cannot claim their actions have substantial public policy significance cannot be sure of protection. Free speech is protected only if a whistle-blower can prove that his or her action was directly related to a particular statute or if a sympathetic court is willing to make a public policy exception to the at-will doctrine. OSHA's Hazard Communication Standard provides access to information identifying the toxic substances present in the workplace, but not to information on exposure levels or the degree of risk to health. The recent wave of legislation has also largely ignored the need for worker associations. Workers employed at work sites where a majority of employees will not vote in favor of union representation or where the employer refuses to sign a contract with the union have effectively no rights of association. This not only prevents collective bargaining but weakens the ability of individual workers to take advantage of the rights guaranteed by statutes.

The Right to Act

The four components of a system of worker representation are the central features of the worker's right to act. Access to information, due process and fairness, free speech, and the right of association are each protected in various ways in the emerging proposals for a strengthened worker-oriented strategy for controlling workplace health and safety hazards.

Access to information is the most securely established part of the current system of workers' rights concerning toxic exposures. Under OSHA regulations, workers have the right to review company records on exposure monitoring and medical surveillance and are entitled to information and training concerning the identity and toxicity of substances used in production processes. Under the Emergency Planning and Community Right to Know Act, workers and community residents have indirect access to information on the quantities of hazardous materials stored in major facilities, the annual volume of emissions into surrounding air and waters, and the extent of accidental spills and discharges. These rights can be exercised by individual workers and do not depend upon collective initiatives or union organizations.

OSHA has proposed new standards that would require firms to conduct exposure monitoring and medical surveillance under certain circumstances.[19] The combination of toxicity information and exposure data allows an estimation of the risks faced by particular workers. Federal legislation has been introduced to establish a mechanism for individually notifying workers who are at exceptionally high risk of illness based on their exposure histories.[20] This has been stalled by opponents who argue that it would serve no clear preventive function but would instead stimulate court claims for retrospective compensation. Notification could serve preventive functions, however, if applied to currently employed workers for whom adequate exposure data are available.

The most important remaining problem surrounding information on toxic substances concerns the worker's ability to understand the data. The basic level of training required for workers under OSHA's Hazard Communication Standard is not sufficient to permit employees to grapple successfully with the risks and alternatives present in the workplace. Individual workers obviously differ in their level of interest and ability to decipher technical data. The most educated and concerned workers are often those most likely to quit, voice objections, or be fired. What is needed, therefore, is a system through which some workers can obtain extra training and be granted special powers to represent their coworkers' interests in these matters.

Free speech concerning workplace hazards and environmental pollution is partially protected under the whistle-blower provisions of the Occupational Safety and Health Act and the major environmental statutes. The protection is incomplete, however, and generic whistle-blower protection legislation has been proposed at the federal level. This legislation would protect individuals who promote the goals of any federal health and safety law in any of three basic ways.[21] It would cover workers disclosing violations of health and safety laws, initiating court proceedings against a violator of these laws, or refusing to participate in any activity that would violate such a law. However, this bill does not guarantee that the best-trained and most-concerned employees are the ones likely to gain access to evidence on violations of health and safety laws. Serendipity would continue to influence which individual had the opportunity to blow the whistle. Once again, the fundamental problem is one of how to centralize and coordinate information on toxic exposures and emissions so that it can be used most effectively.

A very important aspect of due process and fairness guarantees, from the perspective of occupational safety and health, is the worker's right to refuse hazardous work. As described in chapter 3, the current protections for work refusals are very incomplete. The "reasonable person" test leaves the individual worker uncertain of whether new information will later prove his or her fears to be unfounded and the work refusal to be unprotected. Related to the standard of evidence is the issue of how a work refusal by one worker or group of workers affects others. At one extreme, an informed refusal by one worker to perform a hazardous assignment could lead to that task being assigned to a less-informed or less courageous coworker, rather than being made safe. At the other extreme, an uninformed refusal to perform a task that is in fact not hazardous could stop an entire production process and prevent other workers from completing their assignments. A mechanism is needed for coordinating information on hazards and responses by workers at each work site to prevent these problems. The best-trained and most-concerned workers need to be granted special powers to abate imminent hazards, including those afflicting other workers. As documented in chapter 6, the present system gives incentives to management to assign hazardous jobs to those workers least able to take the risks of a work refusal.

The fourth component of a system of worker representation, the right of association, currently is the least protected by law. Nonunion workers who fall outside the collective bargaining framework have essentially no right of association. The worker's need for a right of association with other workers sharing common interests is as strong as ever and, in fact, is growing. As discussed above, each of the other three components of the right to act is significantly limited by the absence of workplace organizations and institutions that can collect hazard data and coordinate appropriate responses.

This form of workplace association has already been developed in embryonic form, through joint labor-management health and safety committees. Such committees are mandated in a majority of union contracts covering large manufacturing firms and in a substantial fraction of contracts covering non-manufacturing work sites. They have been incorporated into law and vested with substantial powers in Canada, England, and Sweden.[22] While these committees vary considerably with respect to their powers, a core set of functions can be identified in the more successful models. On a most basic level, health and safety committees must have access to all information on toxic substances, exposure levels, and health effects. They must be able to gather new information through work-site inspections, reviews of accidents, unusual emissions, and near misses. They should be involved in the supervision of technical health and safety personnel and in the planning of exposure monitoring and medical surveillance. These committees should possess some authority to stop imminently hazardous production processes, thereby replacing individual worker refusals. Underlying all these duties are a set of provisions for special health and safety training, protection against employer retaliation for committee-related activities, and compensation for committee-related work at the member's usual rate of pay.

The right of association is the most controversial of the four elements of the right to act and is the farthest from enactment. The most ambitious version of the right-to-act proposals has been developed by PHILAPOSH and other labor union, environmental, and community groups in New Jersey. Their pioneering work on the right to know has been extended to the right to act and has emerged in the form of proposed legislation that is centered around the establishment of associations both in the workplace and in the broader community.[23] Each facility with twenty or more employees would be required to provide for the selection of Hazard Prevention Advocates who would constitute a Hazard Prevention Committee. Half of the committee members would be designated by management and the other half by the workers, through either their union representative or a direct election (in nonunion facilities). The committees would have all the rights and responsibilities discussed earlier, including access to information, inspection rights, special training and compensation, authority over technical personnel and monitoring programs, plus the right to halt hazardous processes. Decisions would be made by majority vote, with split votes being referred to outside arbitration. The proposed New Jersey legislation would also extend the composition of the EPCRA community committees to include environmental organizations and labor unions and would broaden their powers to include the right to inspect facilities. These community associations would not, however, be granted the right to stop production on their own initiative without bringing in OSHA, EPA, or some other regulatory body.

Conclusion

Each of the major participants in the industrial relations system has helped to establish mechanisms for encouraging worker responses to occupational safety and health hazards. Labor unions have extended their committee structures, grievance and arbitration systems, and collective bargaining activities to cover health and safety. Human resource managers in major nonunion firms have developed programs that encourage employee initiative and cooperation in resolving workplace problems. The national and state legislatures have woven a patchy fabric of statutes that partially protect individual workers against discipline for pursuing socially desirable goals such as control of public health hazards. The new proposals for a guaranteed right to act carry the right-to-know principles to their logical conclusion. Together, these various developments provide an increasingly viable alternative to the "love it or leave it" choice embodied in the exit strategy and the doctrine of employment at will.

9

The Politics of Regulation

Workers pursue both individual exit and collective voice strategies to achieve safer and more healthful conditions. Their private efforts are supported by public statutes and standards that guarantee access to hazard information and protection against discharge without just cause. While effective in many respects, these labor market and legal strategies suffer from two major limitations. First, worker self-help initiatives require hazard information that is often unavailable. Right-to-know standards require employers to divulge data they already possess, but do not require the research that generates new data. Second, worker responses to workplace hazards depend on the availability of alternative job options and possibilities for collective bargaining. Given the concentration of unskilled workers in hazardous jobs and the declining strength of labor unions, there is no guarantee that workplace strategies will produce a socially acceptable degree of risk reduction.

These problems have generated support for a regulatory strategy to control occupational safety and health hazards. As embodied in the Occupational Safety and Health Act of 1970, the regulatory approach focuses on the research, promulgation, and enforcement of standards limiting workplace health risks. The preamble to the statute asserts that workers have a right to a safe and healthy workplace. To the extent that markets generate incentives strong enough to achieve this social goal, no regulatory requirements are necessary. The legislative history and language of the act are, however, deeply imbued with skepticism concerning the effectiveness of market mechanisms.

The 1970 law established two expert agencies to perform research and regulatory functions. The National Institute for Occupational Safety and Health was created within the Department of Health and Human Services to support toxicological, epidemiological, and other research on the health and safety effects of workplace exposures. The Occupational Safety and Health Administration was established within the Department of Labor to promulgate and enforce standards limiting exposures, based in part upon recommendations from NIOSH. If necessary to reduce significant risks to employee health and safety, OSHA is empowered to enforce very stringent and costly exposure limits.

It is instructive to compare this regulatory strategy with the labor market strategies analyzed in previous chapters. In pursuing its goals, the regulatory strategy does not depend in any essential way upon worker exit and voice and thus avoids many of the problems plaguing those initiatives. The workers in a particular firm may be unskilled, nonunion, and speak Spanish rather than English, but OSHA can still force their employer to improve conditions. In establishing standards, moreover, OSHA and NIOSH are not completely dependent upon risk estimates developed by industry but can develop their own data.

Workers and labor unions have seized the opportunities provided by the regulatory structure. Labor unions and other worker-oriented organizations have provided political support for the promulgation and enforcement of standards. Individual workers have used the mechanisms provided by the 1970 act to file complaints concerning violations and participate in OSHA workplace inspections. Management has fought as vigorously against the regulatory agencies, however, as it has against militant workers and labor unions on the shop floor. Virtually every standard promulgated by OSHA during the

1970s was contested, and the agency's enforcement efforts were fought at every turn. With the inauguration of Ronald Reagan in 1981, industry was able to oppose the regulatory strategy from within the regulatory agencies. Budgets for research at NIOSH and enforcement at OSHA were slashed. Many major standards were weakened or revoked completely. By the end of the 1980s, however, the public backlash against this policy of deregulation had become so strong that OSHA began again to consider a broad regulatory effort, albeit of a form different from that pursued in the previous decade. After years on the political defensive, health and safety activists began to support a major legislative strengthening of the original statute.

This chapter analyzes the regulatory strategy for controlling workplace hazards in terms of the ups and downs of the standards-setting process at OSHA since 1970. In order to keep the discussion within manageable proportions, we will focus on standards for controlling occupational exposure to carcinogens, a problem of central concern to the agency since its inception.

OSHA's efforts to control carcinogens can be divided into five major initiatives, which will be examined in chronological order. We begin with the "start-up standards" that were adopted en masse by OSHA in 1971 from the recommendations of private health and safety organizations. This reliance upon private organizations proved to be a source of many serious problems for OSHA. The late 1970s were a time of aggressive standards setting for occupational carcinogens, and the period illustrates not only what a dedicated regulatory agency can achieve, but also the political reaction it can provoke. The high water mark of the regulatory approach to controlling cancer risks was reached with the Generic Carcinogen Policy of 1980, after which OSHA's enthusiasm for exposure limitations declined markedly. The 1983 Hazard Communication Standard, already discussed in previous chapters, was in part an attempt to use OSHA standards to encourage worker initiatives to control occupational carcinogens. The 1989 Air Contaminants Standard, the centerpiece of OSHA's efforts as the 1980s drew to a close, embodied both the worst and the best of the regulatory strategy. At worst, the Air Contaminants Standard symbolized a return to OSHA's earlier reliance on private, industry-dominated organizations that lacked public accountability. At best, it embodied the generic approach to standards setting, with a potential for more comprehensive coverage of occupational carcinogens. The chapter concludes with a consideration of how OSHA's various approaches could be combined into a coherent public health policy for the workplace.

Shadow of the Past: The Start-up Standards

In 1971 OSHA adopted as mandatory exposure limits a large number of voluntary standards developed by private organizations, in particular, by the American Conference of Governmental Industrial Hygienists (ACGIH). Despite its name, the ACGIH is a nongovernmental group with close ties to private industry. It develops Threshold Limit Values (TLVs) for many toxic substances encountered in the industrial workplace. In order to streamline the standards-setting process, OSHA adopted virtually all of the approximately 400 TLVs listed by the ACGIH in 1968 as permissible exposure limits without even a cursory evaluation of their adequacy.[1]

The adoption of the TLVs made OSHA dependent upon the ACGIH and its TLV-setting process, both of which evolved during the preregulatory period, when industry was virtually the sole source of research on occupational health. The ACGIH asserted that the TLVs were based upon health data alone, to the exclusion of economic considerations. The TLVs were said to be "thresholds," in the sense of representing "conditions under which it is believed that nearly all workers may be repeatedly exposed day after day without adverse effect."[2] This was an inaccurate and misleading portrayal. In the years prior to the passage of the 1970 Occupational Safety and Health Act, industry was under no obligation to divulge data it had developed from epidemiological studies of worker groups, from toxicological studies of animals in laboratory experiments, or from industrial hygiene studies of prevalent exposure levels. The ACGIH depended upon the collaboration of industry representatives for the development of the TLVs and gradually granted these representatives direct responsibility for reviewing particular substances. Not surprisingly, corporate industrial hygienists and physicians were most familiar with the substances produced by their employers, and so a pattern developed in which industry experts were given responsibility for recommending safe thresholds for chemicals in which they had a strong financial stake. This conflict of interest became accentuated in the 1970s when, partly as a result of OSHA's adoption of the TLVs, corporate involvement in the TLV-setting process deepened. Representatives of the Dow Chemical and Dupont corporations constituted two of the four members of the new ACGIH subcommittee on carcinogenic substances. This subcommittee was in charge of establishing the TLVs for widely used Dow carcinogens such as vinyl chloride and methyl chloride and Dupont carcinogens such as dimethyl sulphate, lead chromate, and MOCA.[3]

The TLVs were buttressed by an ACGIH publication, "Documentation of the Threshold Limit Values," that purported to be a comprehensive review of the relevant scientific literature on each substance. This claim is highly questionable. Fully 104 of the approximately 600 TLVs listed in the 1986 documentation were substantiated solely or primarily by unpublished corporate communications and reports.[4] The most solidly established TLVs, presumably, were those for which there existed published epidemiological studies. An analysis of the available epidemiological studies referenced in the 1986 documentation found a marked disparity between the findings actually reported in the studies and the inferences drawn from the studies by the TLV committee.[5] Despite the claim that the TLVs represented exposure thresholds below which almost all workers would be safe, the vast majority of the published studies reported significant adverse effects at exposures equal to or less than the level subsequently chose as the TLV.

The TLVs did not exhibit any consistent statistical association with the exposure level at which no significant health effects were reported; some studies reported no adverse effects at exposure levels above the TLV, while others reported many adverse effects at exposure levels below the TLV. The TLVs did, however, reveal a very strong and consistent statistical association with the exposure levels reported as prevalent in industry. This suggests that, contrary to the assertions of the ACGIH, economic factors played a dominant role in the choice of TLVs. The inadequacy of the TLVs has become more and more evident. Between 1987 and 1989, for example, over thirty studies were published documenting adverse health effects at exposure levels below the TLV.[6]

The limitations inherent in the TLVs themselves were compounded by the manner in which OSHA translated them into permissible exposure limits. The TLV list adopted by OSHA in 1971 had identified a number of substances as carcinogenic and recommended exposures be eliminated completely. These recommendations were not included in the body of the TLV list but rather in a special appendix. Relying upon a legal technicality, OSHA claimed that this appendix was not part of the TLV list that it was authorized to promulgate into standards, and hence excluded these substances.[7] Therefore, despite the fact that concern for occupational carcinogens had played a large role in the passage of its enabling legislation, OSHA in its start-up period did not regulate any chemicals based upon evidence of cancer effects.

Carcinogen Regulation in the 1970s

After this slow start, OSHA focused much of its standards-setting energies during the 1970s on carcinogens, including vinyl chloride and acrylonitrile in plastics manufacturing, inorganic arsenic and coke oven emissions in metal mining and milling, benzene in petroleum refining and petrochemicals, and asbestos in a wide range of industries. This regulatory vigor elicited an equally vigorous response from industry, manifested initially in court challenges to particular standards and eventually in a political strategy to replace the existing OSHA leadership with one more sensitive to corporate concerns.

Two issues surfaced with regularity at each court challenge to OSHA's carcinogen regulations: scientific uncertainty and compliance costs. One debate focused on the validity of extrapolating to current exposure levels from historical epidemiological evidence and from laboratory evidence on cancer effects in animals. This involved "science policy" questions such as whether there existed a threshold of safety for carcinogens and whether animal evidence was predictive of human carcinogenesis. Industry repeatedly argued that the unresolved scientific uncertainties were reason to defer regulation, an ironic position given that industry refusals to gather and divulge exposure and health effects data were responsible for much of the uncertainty.[8]

The second debate revolved around the proper role in regulatory decision making for estimates of industry compliance costs. The 1970 statute is very ambiguous in this matter, declaring that OSHA "shall set the standard which most adequately assures, to the extent feasible, on the basis of the best available evidence, that no employee will suffer material impairment of health or functional capacity."[9] In this passage, "to the extent feasible" could easily be interpreted in a purely technical, noneconomic sense, and was so interpreted by labor unions and public interest groups in the proceedings surrounding the promulgation of the 1972 asbestos standard. OSHA, however, argued that economic, as well as technological, feasibility was implied in the legislation.[10] OSHA developed an interpretation of economic feasibility according to which compliance costs relative to total profits should not be so high as to drive a significant number of firms out of business.[11] It explicitly rejected cost-benefit analysis, despite the recommendations of administration economists and the vociferous support for such analyses by industry. In minimizing the role of economic considerations, however, OSHA was swimming against the tide of the times. Beginning with President Ford and continuing with Presidents Carter and Reagan, ever more stringent requirements were placed upon regulatory agencies to evaluate and justify industry's compliance costs.[12]

Frustrated with the continual rehashing of these two debates in every substance-specific standard, OSHA focused its efforts on the development of a generic approach to cancer regulation. The 1980 Generic Carcinogen Policy established a categorization system for confirmed or suspected carcinogens, with immediate regulatory action proposed for substances falling into the highest priority category. This category would include substances that increased the incidence of tumors in humans or in suitably designed laboratory experiments on animals. From the universe of substances falling into the highest priority category, OSHA would identify ten substances for comprehensive standards setting at any one time. These standards would include requirements for exposure limits, exposure monitoring, medical surveillance, container labeling, and worker training. The exposure limits were to be set at the lowest economically feasible level.

The Generic Carcinogen Policy was weakened almost as soon as it was promulgated. In July 1980, the U.S. Supreme Court upheld a lower court decision to throw out OSHA's benzene standard, on the grounds that the agency had not proven that exposures at the level regulated by the standard posed a "significant risk" to employees.[13] This ruling implied that any standard not demonstrating significant risk would be overturned. The type of evidence sufficient to qualify chemicals for the highest priority category in OSHA's Generic Carcinogen Policy did not demonstrate significant risk without further analysis. In January 1981 OSHA issued a revised policy that mandated a two-step approach to the categorization of individual carcinogens.[14] For each substance falling into the highest priority category, an assessment would be made of whether current exposure levels constituted a significant risk.

Chemicals considered to pose such a risk would then be regulated down to the lowest feasible level, as provided in the original policy.

Of greater import for the Generic Carcinogen Policy was the inauguration of Ronald Reagan several days later. OSHA's cancer policy was listed by the new administration's Task Force on Regulatory Relief as one of the first twenty-seven regulations to be reconsidered due to their economic costs. In March 1981 the policy was withdrawn in order to permit OSHA to "address alternatives that had not been fully considered." The policy remained in abeyance from then on and has never been used as the basis for standards setting at OSHA.

The Generic Carcinogen Policy represents OSHA's most aggressive initiative directed at occupational carcinogens. It embodies all of the most health-protective assumptions about the biological process of carcinogenesis. Of greatest importance, it declares that regulation should proceed for those chemicals where there exists laboratory evidence of cancer effects in animals but not yet epidemiological evidence of cancer effects in humans. The policy also weighs the costs and benefits of regulation in a manner strongly oriented toward regulation. OSHA's definition of a "feasible" level is a highly stringent one. While not unique in its adoption of this concept of feasibility, the Generic Carcinogen Policy stands out in its effort to extend the principle expeditiously to a sweeping array of chemicals.

Substance-Specific Carcinogen Regulation in the 1980s

With the abandonment of the Generic Carcinogen Policy, OSHA continued to promulgate substance-specific standards in the 1980s, but with even less success than during the previous decade. The battles of the 1970s had produced three legal and institutional barriers to aggressive regulation of occupational carcinogens. First, the Supreme Court's "significant risk" doctrine required the agency to perform a detailed quantitative risk assessment for each candidate carcinogen. Second, industry concern about compliance costs produced an increasingly rigorous set of requirements for the agency to estimate the economic impact of each proposed regulation. Third, the regulatory strategy of the 1970s raised OSHA to an unenviable position of high visibility and vulnerability with respect to the Office of Management and Budget, which interpreted its own role as one of reining in a regulatory process gone amok.[15]

Given these impediments and the general antiregulatory mood of the Reagan and Bush administrations, it was perhaps remarkable that OSHA completed any cancer regulations at all. Its record of achievement during the 1980s was quite modest. It consisted of leftover business from the previous decade in the form of the revised benzene and asbestos standards, plus the promulgation of new regulations governing ethylene oxide and formaldehyde. Two features characterize these substance-specific regulations. First, they cover substances for which there exists epidemiological evidence of carcinogenicity in worker populations. This constitutes an implicit rejection of the guiding principle of the Generic Carcinogen Policy, which was designed to stimulate regulation of substances for which only animal evidence was available. The second salient feature of the substance-specific regulations is their relative stringency. The permissible exposure limit was reduced by 98% for ethylene oxide, 90% for asbestos and benzene, and 66% for formaldehyde.

The 1983 Hazard Communication Standard as a Carcinogen Regulation

In many ways the most important regulation promulgated by OSHA during the 1980s was the Hazard Communication Standard, already discussed in chapter 7. Although the Hazard Communication Standard does not focus on carcinogens, it treats these substances differently from noncarcinogens and imposes important new obligations upon producers and users. Its ultimate efficacy in reducing rates of work-related cancer will depend, however, on worker exit and voice responses to the newly available risk information.

The Hazard Communication Standard is a "performance standard" that delegates to management the responsibility to decide which substances are hazardous. Nevertheless, the standard does provide a minimum of substances that must be covered. This includes chemicals listed as carcinogens by the International Association for Research on Cancer (IARC) of the World Health Organization or by the National Toxicology Program (NTP) of the U.S. Department of Health and Human Services.[16] In addition, chemicals must be designated as potential carcinogens and included in worker training programs if they have produced evidence of carcinogenicity in well-conducted animal studies. According to one estimate, these provisions mandate inclusion of 416 substances based on the IARC and NTP documents plus an additional 2,260 substances with laboratory evidence of carcinogenicity that have not been classified by IARC or NTP.[17] This broad scope is reminiscent of the Generic Carcinogen Policy, since it places animal data front and center in establishing which substances will be treated as occupational carcinogens.

While similar in scope to the Generic Carcinogen Policy, the Hazard Communication Standard differs markedly in terms of regulatory requirements. It imposes no permissible exposure limits, much less limits that are the lowest feasible short of ruining the industry. The Hazard Communication Standard imposes four duties on producers and users of toxic substances. Chemical manufacturers must prepare Material Safety Data Sheets on each of their products, including information on the precise chemical identity, related health hazards, signs and symptoms of exposure, precautions for safe handling, generally applicable control measures, and emergency spill procedures. Manufacturers must also prepare shipping labels, which refer back to the MSDS. All employers, not just chemical manufacturers, must prepare written hazard communication programs that list hazardous materials used at their work sites, and must conduct training sessions to educate employees concerning the identity, use, and control of those substances.

The 1989 Air Contaminants Standard as a Carcinogen Regulation

Dissatisfaction continued to grow on all sides concerning the slow pace of standards setting at OSHA. As of 1988, only twenty-four toxic substances had been regulated, if one ignores the exposure limits adopted in 1971 based upon the ACGIH Threshold Limit Values. Meanwhile, the ACGIH was continuing to adopt new TLVs and had lowered many of the TLVs for previously covered substances. The growing disparity between OSHA's standards and these revised TLVs was a source of considerable embarrassment for the agency. OSHA saw an opportunity to blunt some of the criticism by adopting the 1986–87 TLV list as mandatory standards. Despite the extensive evidence on the failings of the TLV-setting process, OSHA decided to repeat history.

In January 1989, OSHA promulgated the Air Contaminants Standard, lowering the permissible exposure limits for 212 substances regulated under the 1971 start-up provisions and imposing new limits for 164 substances not previously regulated by the agency.[18] Given the legal developments of the intervening years, OSHA could not simply adopt the 1986–87 TLVs with the alacrity with which it had adopted their 1968 counterparts. In a lengthy preamble published in the *Federal Register*, OSHA argued that it had analyzed each substance and determined that the risks being reduced were "significant" and that the costs of compliance were "feasible." Compared with the extensive epidemiological and economic studies performed for the substance-specific standards, these significant risk and feasibility evaluations can be described most charitably as streamlined. Exposure data were obtained from the limited number of measurements taken by OSHA compliance officers over the years and were supplemented by telephone interviews with management personnel who were asked whether exposure levels in their plants exceeded the TLVs. Acute chemical illness data were obtained from the U.S. Bureau of Labor Statistics, although many of the health effects caused by exposure to substances regulated under the standard would not appear in the BLS statistics. In contrast with the substance-specific standards, the Air Contaminants Standard received strong support from major corporate interests and quick approval from the Office of Management and Budget.

Blessed by the traditional opponents of regulation, the Air Contaminants Standard was damned by regulation's traditional proponents. The AFL-CIO voiced its approval of the generic approach to standards setting but argued that the new standard should apply to more substances, that the permissible exposure limits should be stricter for many substances, that the standard should require exposure monitoring and medical surveillance, and that the standard should cover the agricultural, construction, and maritime industries, which had been excluded.[19] What raised the ire of the labor unions the most, however, was the principle of relying upon the industry-oriented ACGIH in lieu of the National Institute for Occupational Safety and Health, despite the clear statutory role for NIOSH in OSHA standards setting.

The implications of ignoring NIOSH in favor of ACGIH were clearly evident in the public hearings held by OSHA when the standard was initially proposed. NIOSH presented over 4,000 pages of written testimony and supporting documents as part of its criticism of the TLV-based Permissible Exposure Limits (PELs). NIOSH had previously developed numerical Recommended Exposure Limits (RELs) for 50 of these substances. OSHA's new standards permitted exposures at levels up to 1,000 times higher than those recommended by NIOSH. NIOSH presented epidemiological and toxicological evidence on an additional 42 substances that had been excluded from the Air Contaminants Standard, due to the absence of TLVs.[20]

OSHA's treatment of carcinogens in the Air Contaminants Standard was particularly difficult to justify. Of the 326 substances affected by the standard, 78 were considered to be carcinogens by NIOSH, NTP, and/or IARC. Only 11 of these were classified as carcinogens by OSHA, however, because of its heavy reliance on the ACGIH TLVs. OSHA decided to base a particular exposure limit upon cancer risk if the ACGIH had designated the substance a carcinogen and also had established a numerical TLV. The carcinogens not meeting these criteria were regulated in the Air Contaminants Standard based upon risks of noncancer health effects.[21]

This reliance upon the TLVs resulted in both internal inconsistency with respect to the stringency of particular exposure limits and external inconsistency with the recommendations of scientific organizations. For 7 substances regulated as carcinogens, the OSHA PEL equals the ACGIH TLV, for 3 substances the PEL is stricter than the TLV, and for 1 substance the PEL is less strict than the TLV. For 8 of the 11 substances regulated as carcinogens, OSHA obtained risk assessments of the expected number of cancer cases per 1,000 exposed workers at the new permissible exposure limits. In its substance-specific cancer regulations, OSHA had previously argued that any risk above 1 in 1,000 was significant. In the Air Contaminants Standard, however, the majority of the risks exceed this level. The residual risks ranged up to 11.3 cancers per 1,000 exposed workers for perchlorethylene, a solvent widely used in the dry cleaning industry; 12.0 per 1,000 workers for p-toluidine, a chemical intermediary used in the production of dyes, rubber products, and pesticides; and 40.0 per 1,000 workers for vinyl bromide, an important raw material in plastics manufacturing.

The external inconsistency between the Air Contaminants Standard and the recommendations of scientific organizations with responsibilities for evaluating cancer risks is even more striking. Fully 67 of the substances with permissible exposure limits based solely on noncancer health risks were identified as confirmed or probable human carcinogens by

NIOSH, NTP, and/or IARC. The epidemiological evidence of cancer effects was particularly strong for benzene-soluble coal tar pitch, soluble or inorganic nickel, nickel carbonyl, benzo(a)pyrene, hydrazine, dimethylhydrazine, propylene imine, and MOCA. An additional 68 substances previously identified as occupational carcinogens by NIOSH and/or NTP were excluded from the Air Contaminants Standard altogether due to its reliance on ACGIH. These included confirmed human carcinogens such as insoluble hexavalent chromium compounds and fumes and dusts from nickel sulfide roasting.[22]

Regulatory policy at OSHA seemed to have come full circle in twenty years. After controversial efforts during the late 1970s to force the development of new products and processes, OSHA in 1989 fell back upon the ACGIH Threshold Limit Values from which it had started. Nothing better illustrates the strength of employers in defeating occupational health initiatives. Industry opposed the substance-specific carcinogen regulations, weakening some and overturning others. It paralyzed the Generic Carcinogen Policy. After proposing a purely voluntary approach to worker training, it initiated the Hazard Communication Standard as a means for preempting stronger state and local statutes. It supported the Air Contaminants Standard as a legitimation of the informal and industry-oriented evaluation of occupational health risks that prevailed in the years prior to 1970. The economic power of employers on the shop floor and in the labor market, documented in previous chapters, seems to pale compared with the political power of employers documented here.

This appearance of industry invincibility can be deceiving. The regulatory strategy embodied in the 1970 Occupational Safety and Health Act has certainly fallen short of its most optimistic expectations. But the basic principle of the 1970 legislation, namely, that occupational health is a matter of legitimate public concern rather than a private matter between individual employers and individual employees, has become firmly established. As the third decade of occupational health regulation unfolds, a new approach is combining elements from both the regulatory focus on permissible exposure limits and the labor market focus on information and worker participation.

Conclusion

Considerable bitterness remains among management, labor, and others concerning the history of regulation and deregulation at OSHA. The prospects for the near future are for continued acrimony and regulatory paralysis. For the longer term, however, possibilities are emerging for a less conflictual and ultimately more effective governmental approach to occupational safety and health problems. As emphasized throughout this book, workers pursue both private and public strategies to control workplace hazards. Private strategies include quitting and collective bargaining. Public strategies include appeals for judicial review of personnel policies and the promulgation of permissible exposure limits. OSHA's traditional focus is on the last of these. Its overall impact is potentially greatest, however, when available resources are allocated so as to support all four strategies.

The most important innovation in OSHA's policy since the 1970s has been the increase in public support for private worker initiatives. The right to know and, to a lesser degree, the right to act have been strengthened by OSHA's standards. This trend is continuing in the form of a debate over how OSHA can encourage the creation of labor-management health and safety committees at union and nonunion work sites.[23] OSHA has also begun to reform its process for developing permissible exposure limits. The 1989 Air Contaminants Standard signaled a desire on OSHA's part to streamline its system. Reliance upon the ACGIH proved a costly mistake, but the basic principle of generic standards setting for toxic substances has received support from both ends of the political spectrum. One important possibility is for industry and labor to compromise and allow OSHA to speed up the process of regulation in exchange for less stringent reductions in permissible exposures for particular substances. This exchange of depth for breadth would bring more hazards under OSHA's active purview while allowing the reductions in exposure limits to accompany, rather than precede, cost-reducing technological innovations.[24]

The next major component of OSHA's overall approach to workplace hazards is its proposal for generic exposure monitoring and medical surveillance standards.[25] If promulgated and successfully enforced, these standards will provide data essential for both private and public strategies in the future. Most obviously, monitoring and surveillance requirements would fill the information gap in the worker's right to know about workplace hazards by supplying exposure and health effects data for particular workplaces and individual workers. They would counter the employers' current disincentives to evaluate working conditions. The monitoring and surveillance standards could potentially encourage new exit and voice initiatives. The exposure and health effects data would also enhance the regulatory strategy by providing a solid basis for ensuring compliance with permissible exposure limits and for evaluating the technical and economic feasibility of further reductions in exposures.

OSHA has a range of tools at its disposal. It can impose permissible exposure limits that directly control hazards, support exit and voice initiatives through standards guaranteeing hazard communication and the worker's right to refuse hazardous work, and require exposure monitoring and medical surveillance to strengthen the next round of exposure limits and worker initiatives. The historical record proves than none of these tools by itself is adequate for achieving the legislated goals of the agency. Direct regulation of toxic exposures cannot ensure safe and healthy working conditions in the absence of an informed and active work force. Public support for worker exit and voice strategies cannot achieve socially acceptable risk reductions in the absence of solidly researched and enforced exposure limits. Exposure monitoring and medical surveillance will only contribute to improved health when used as the basis for exposure limits and worker training. In its third decade, OSHA can combine the three approaches into a more coherent and effective public policy for controlling safety hazards and toxic substances in the workplace.

10

The Means and the Ends

In seeking to reduce their risks of occupational injury and illness, workers can pursue any of several strategies. These strategies can be primarily individual or primarily collective, mainly private or mainly public. Workers can rely upon their own skills and the opportunities provided by a competitive labor market, on their fellow workers and the power of collective bargaining, on an attorney and a jury of their peers, or on a regulatory agency and the enforcement of permissible exposure limits. As documented throughout this book, these strategies have both strengths and weaknesses. What are the advantages and disadvantages of each? Are they substitutes for one other, capable of doing the job alone and hindered by interference from the others? Or are they complements, each limited in what it can achieve alone and most effective when coordinated with the others? This chapter compares the four strategies for controlling work-related hazards: individual job shopping, collective action through unionization, pursuit of individual rights in the legal arena, and direct control of public health hazards through governmental regulation. This evaluation of the means will also clarify the ends. What, fundamentally, is the goal of public policy in occupational safety and health?

The Exit Strategy:
Job Shopping and Consumer Sovereignty

The exit model of worker behavior underlies the analysis of quit rates in chapter 2, compensating wage differentials in chapter 5, and the sorting of workers between hazardous and safe jobs in chapter 6. Labor market competition between workers for jobs with the best characteristics and between firms for workers with the best skills leads to higher wages in hazardous jobs. In its pure form the theory of compensating differentials requires that workers be fully informed as to the hazards present in each job, something obviously at odds with the facts. But the theory gains in plausibility when linked to the exit model of worker learning and job shopping. Workers who are not initially informed gradually learn about some of the risks and move to the safer jobs unless offered appropriate compensation. Employers with hazardous jobs face higher hiring costs, training costs, and quit rates than employers with safe jobs. They can reduce these turnover-related costs by raising wages or by improving working conditions. Well-managed firms seek to balance safety improvements, hazard pay premiums, and hiring and training expenditures so as to minimize total production costs.

Exit responses to hazard information motivate employers to invest in safer work practices because they offer the possibility of recouping those investments through reduced hazard pay and reduced turnover costs. Exit responses provide incentives for exactly the right level of safety investments, if one accepts the normative framework underlying the theory. While workers prefer safe conditions to hazardous conditions, they also prefer high wages to low wages. The key question concerns how the total compensation package is to be divided between wages and improvements in working conditions. The normative framework underlying the exit model assumes that the appropriate allocation of the compensation package is the one desired by the exposed workers themselves; any other allocation would be paternalistic. Employers can obtain the greatest employee satisfaction at the least cost by experimenting with different mixes of wages and improved working conditions to find the one most preferred by their workers. In this sense, turnover functions as a signal to employers concerning their employees' preferences for improved wages or improved working conditions.

This interpretation of hazard-related turnover is part of a broader perspective on the labor market and the economy as a whole. In a dynamic economy, new products and new processes are constantly being developed, with subsequent changes in the demand for labor. New jobs open up while old jobs are eliminated. It is essential for workers to move to positions in which their skills are best utilized. In a market economy, this mobility is largely assured by worker quits. Firms needing new employees offer higher wages or better working conditions in order to induce workers to move. The self-interested pursuit of the best wages and working conditions by individual workers serves the social need for labor to move to its most productive uses. Needless to say, not all labor mobility is voluntary. A sizeable minority of workers leave their jobs because of layoff or discharge. Even here, however, the ultimate cause is often a lower productivity in the worker's previous job than elsewhere in the economy.

Seen in this light, worker exit responses to information on hazards is one of society's means for exerting pressure on employers to improve working conditions. If the productivity of labor in hazardous firms is not sufficient to permit wage premiums that adequately compensate workers for the additional risk, then those firms will close down. Turnover can also improve productivity, by creating a better match between working conditions and worker preferences. Individual workers differ considerably in the weight they place on particular working conditions, such as risks to health and safety. Labor market mobility allows those most averse to hazard to shift to the safer, but lower-paying, jobs, while those least averse to hazard shift to the more dangerous, but better-paying, positions. This improved match between working conditions and worker preferences presumably promotes job satisfaction. While workers in hazardous jobs are more likely to report dissatisfaction with their jobs than are workers in safe jobs, as evidenced in chapter 4, the difference is much smaller than it would be if there were no possibilities for job shopping.

Turnover not only achieves socially desirable goals but achieves them with a frugal use of resources. Not all workers must be willing and able to quit hazardous jobs in order for employers to recognize the need to pay higher wages or improve working conditions. In this, employers are analogous to producers of consumer goods, who must tailor price and quality to the most discerning shoppers. While many consumers will not bother to read package labels and compare prices among similar products, some consumers will. Firms usually cannot establish one combination of price and quality for comparison shoppers and another for those not willing or able to compare; thus they offer the best price and quality to all. From a social point of view, this spillover effect is highly desirable, since it conserves the time of those shoppers not comparing alternative products. In the labor market, workers unaware or indifferent to workplace hazards will reap spillover benefits from the exit responses of their coworkers.

The most important characteristic of the exit strategy for controlling occupational hazards, in the eyes of its proponents, is not its efficiency but rather its compatibility with a core set of philosophical values. In principle, the exit strategy consists of voluntary choices by individual workers and managers without coercion from the government or organized groups. No worker is forced to accept a hazardous job, and no worker is prevented from quitting one he or she has accepted. Conversely, no employer is forced to hire any particular worker, and no employer is prevented from discharging a worker whose services are no longer desired. Each individual looks after his or her own interests while respecting the rights of others. Socially desired goals are obtained without need for altruism. This is the labor market analogue to the decentralized control over the price and quality of consumer goods produced by market competition; in economic theory, decentralized control is embodied in the principle of "consumer sovereignty." This libertarian framework has strong roots in American political and ethical philosophy and shapes many of the basic institutions of this society. It is both individualistic in temperament and contractarian in structure.[1] Any process that is voluntarily and noncoercively agreed to is considered fair, and the outcomes that flow from fair processes are themselves considered fair. The paradigmatic social relationship is the contract, a mutually advantageous agreement between self-interested individuals. Groups are viewed with skepticism and government with hostility. Mutual advantage through market relationships creates a basic harmony of interests among individuals that obviates the need for collective voice mechanisms and politics.

Limits on the Exit Strategy:
Noisy Signals and Coerced Consent

Individualism and antipathy to public initiative dominated the American cultural landscape in the age when firms were small, labor was mobile, and the frontier appeared to offer opportunities for the enterprising and the diligent. The dominant ethos of the twentieth century has been more sympathetic to the principles of social responsibility and the politics of social legislation. The National Labor Relations Act of 1935, the Civil Rights Act of 1964, the Occupational Safety and Health Act of 1970, and judicial erosion of the employment-at-will doctrine have been part of a broad effort to strengthen the position of individual workers and citizens using collective and political means. The ideology of individual responsibility and the competitive marketplace re-emerged during the 1970s, however, and was embraced by the Reagan administration. The theory of compensating differentials, hazard-related quits, and labor market incentives for hazard abatement provided the theoretical rationale for the subsequent policies of deregulation.[2] It is particularly important, therefore, to consider the limitations as well as the advantages of individual and private worker strategies for achieving a healthy workplace.

The efficacy of worker job shopping in generating compensation and prevention incentives depends on the clarity with which the exit signal is heard by the employer. The mere fact that an employer has difficulties attracting and retaining employees does not necessarily motivate an appropriate response. Quits occur for many reasons totally unrelated to working conditions, and it is not easy for employers to discern the motivation for any particular set of quit decisions. It is also quite difficult for the employer to decide whether the best response to turnover is an increase in wages, an improvement in working conditions, or a resigned acceptance of higher recruitment and training costs. In short, a signal can be heard only to the extent that it stands out against the background noise. For many employers, particularly those with smaller work forces, where turnover does not have an obvious pattern, the level of labor market noise is high indeed.

Even if the exit signal were audible to the employer, it is not clear that it would encourage the best response, regardless of whether this is interpreted in terms of the employer's self-interest or in terms of the social advantages derived from labor market competition. One of the salient facts emphasized by proponents of the exit strategy is that workers vary greatly in their awareness of and concern for working conditions. But if the preferences of workers likely to quit their jobs are different from the preferences of workers unlikely to quit, then the quit signal is conveying information about the wrong set of preferences. Employers are ultimately concerned with the satisfaction and productivity of the employees who stay, not with the satisfaction and productivity of the employees who leave.

The workers most likely to quit are those most concerned for health and safety, those who ordinarily would provide the leadership for shop floor efforts to achieve better working conditions. Turnover eliminates the natural leadership and thereby weakens the ability of the remaining workers to express their preferences in a meaningful way. Indeed, employers may consciously encourage turnover on the part of the most aware and articulate workers, precisely to forestall the spread of concern for hazards. This encouragement may be more or less subtle; the strong association between hazard levels and rates of discharges reported in chapter 4 should not be forgotten.[3] More generally, exit strategies provide no mechanism for storing the hazard information obtained by individual workers. If the most informed workers quit, then only the least informed remain. A process of "musical chairs" can be imagined, in which workers systematically quit the jobs whose hazards are known to them and accept the jobs whose hazards are unknown to them.[4]

The claim that exit strategies are frugal in their use of social resources is open to dispute. Many of the most important worker skills in the modern economy are learned on the job and are specific to particular work sites. Job switching wastes this investment in on-the-job training. The exit model of worker behavior assumes that workers are usually not familiar with job characteristics before being hired but learn about those characteristics over the course of employment. Becoming familiar with job-specific hazards and learning job-specific skills thus occurs over the same period. Quitting, the desired response to one form of learning, is precisely the undesired response to the other. In the U.S. economy, quit rates decline sharply with worker tenure. The notion that subtle occupational hazards will generate much by way of quit signals is fanciful. It is interesting to recall the quite inconsistent pattern of statistical evidence concerning hazard and quits presented in chapter 2. Some hazards are quickly recognized and may well produce quits before workers have accumulated on-the-job training and promotions, while other hazards are more subtle and are only recognized after the costs of quitting have become prohibitive. In such cases, workers may pursue voice strategies, but this is not part of the exit paradigm.

The philosophical virtues of the exit strategy are quite thin. The libertarian view of the labor market interprets buyers and sellers of labor services as similar to buyers and sellers of other commodities, such as vegetables in an open-air market. The notion that individual workers seeking jobs in the modern labor market are equal in bargaining power to the huge corporations with whom they contract is difficult to swallow. The economic and political power of management has been evidenced throughout this book, in the decline of union representation (chapter 2), in resistance to union health and safety programs (chapter 3), in discharges of workers in hazardous jobs (chapter 4), in the reorganization of production to reduce dependence on skilled workers (chapters 5 and 6), in the concealment of hazard information and opposition to disclosure requirements (chapter 7), in efforts to limit the worker's right to act on workplace hazards (chapter 8), and in political campaigns to eviscerate government regulation (chapter 9). Libertarian views of social justice traditionally begin with a formalized model of rational and self-interested individuals making mutually advantageous transactions in the marketplace and end by defending a set of social and labor market outcomes in which the winners and losers are only too easy to identify.[5]

Exit strategies on the part of workers with the best job options produce the labor market sorting identified in chapters 5 and 6. Contrary to simple versions of the doctrine of compensating differentials, hazardous jobs pay low wages, not high wages. Individual contracting between employers and employees provides incentives for firms to reduce skill requirements in hazardous positions and to staff those jobs disproportionately with socially disadvantaged workers who have few alternatives. While workers enjoy the liberty to accept or reject a hazardous job at the outset, they must renounce the liberty to control working conditions once they accept employment. As documented in chapter 5, the process of production in hazardous jobs relies heavily on rules, regulations, and management authority rather than on worker participation in decision making.

The greatest irony of the exit paradigm concerns its libertarian insistence upon the natural harmony of interests in a market economy and society. Each individual does have an interest in upholding a social structure that permits cooperation and the division of labor. This formal harmony of interests will produce actual harmony in behavior only if agreement is possible as to how the economic benefits from social cooperation are to be divided. Under the basic assumptions of the libertarian framework, no reliance can be placed on altruism or appeals to communitarian values. The self-interest that motivates individuals to enter into market transactions also motivates them to use force and fraud to appropriate the largest possible portion of the common benefits. The relatively unregulated labor markets of the eighteenth and nineteenth centuries were characterized by bitter and violent struggles between employers and employees of a kind rarely seen today, after a century of nonlibertarian social policy.

The Voice Strategy: Collective Bargaining and Workplace Democracy

The voice strategy embodied in labor unions and collective bargaining performs the same compensation and prevention functions as individual exit strategies. As described in chapter 3, labor unions engage in a range of activities concerning workplace health and safety, including safety training, defense of workers disciplined for refusing hazardous tasks, collective bargaining, and health and safety committees. The prevention of workplace injuries and illnesses is pursued directly via the negotiation of work practices, dispute resolution mechanisms, provision of safety equipment, and environmental protections. Financial compensation for workers exposed to hazards or suffering injuries and illnesses is achieved through hazard pay premiums, supplemental disability pay, and support in filing Workers' Compensation claims and tort lawsuits. As always, these compensation mechanisms provide an additional financial incentive for management to invest in prevention.

In its own way, moreover, the voice strategy is frugal in the social resources it requires. Not all workers benefiting from union health and safety programs need to be actively involved in their unions, and many need not be union members at all. Most unions rely upon a minority of the work force to provide the energy and resourcefulness to challenge management prerogatives. Nonunion firms often adopt the most innovative union programs as a means of preventing unionization or achieving a more satisfied and productive work force even in the absence of serious threat of unionization.[6] The nonunion human resources management style described in chapter 8 owes much to labor union innovations in grievance procedures, health and safety committees, and other aspects of industrial relations.

Historically in the United States, trade unionism and collective bargaining were conceptualized as the solution to recurrent labor market conflict and episodic class warfare. The passage of the National Labor Relations Act of 1935 symbolized the acceptance by broad sectors of management as well as by public opinion that collective worker action was inevitable and needed to be incorporated into the social and political mainstream. The newly established industrial unions of the New Deal era served to contain shop floor militancy and socialist politics. The "business unionism" that emerged provided a labor market basis for the economic stability and growth of the postwar period. Industrywide collective bargaining produced fairer treatment of employees and higher overall productivity.[7] The potential for productivity-decreasing industrial conflict in hazardous industries was extensively documented in chapter 4.

While the exit strategy embodies the philosophy of individualism and consumer sovereignty, the voice strategy embodies an alternative philosophy of worker cooperation and industrial democracy. The libertarian emphasis on the formal equality of sellers and buyers in the labor market is rejected in favor of an emphasis on the actual inequality of individual workers and large employers. For all their differences, the various strands of the trade union movement embrace some version of the theme that the interests of the individual worker are best achieved through unity of action with other workers. On this point the conservative craft-oriented unionists of the American Federation of Labor were as adamant as the socialist and communist activists in the Congress of Industrial Organizations. If pressed for a philosophical articulation of their perspective, most American trade unionists today would accept the basic market institutions but would insist on the necessity of a countervailing power to balance the strength of employers. The unionized industrial relations framework presupposes no underlying harmony of interests between management and labor, but rather an institutionalized and contained divergence of interests.

If unionism emphasizes voice over exit as the appropriate worker response to health hazards and other workplace problems, it maintains an emphasis on the fairness of voluntary agreements and the outcomes of those agreements. Contracts between individual workers and individual employers are viewed as subject to considerable coercion, given the worker's inability to subsist for a long time without wage income. But contracts between organized workers and organized employers are viewed as fair, and their outcomes as socially appropriate. Indeed, the primary focus of labor unions in the United States is the collectively bargained contract. Although a different version of contractarianism than the libertarian one embodied in the exit paradigm, this union focus is contractarian nonetheless. Labor unions appeal to public policy to establish and maintain the basic institutional structure of industrial relations, but vociferously resist attempts by government to question the outcomes of the bargaining process.

The voice strategy is strong in precisely those areas in which the exit strategy is weak. Voice mechanisms can easily be interpreted as their own form of signal to employers concerning employee preferences, but they take a quite different form than the exit signal. The signal embodied in hazard-related quits struggles to be heard against the background noise of labor market turnover. Its message is ambiguous; it does not indicate the cause of the turnover and is distorted by its focus on the preferences of the mobile employees. In contrast, union voice mechanisms are more explicit as to the exact cause of the discontent and focus on the preferences of the stable employees who tend to dominate union politics. Union grievance mechanisms and safety committees are usually quite articulate in presenting the matters of greatest concern to the rank and file. Not only a vehicle for the expression of discontent, union voice mechanisms can serve as a source of ideas for solutions.

Voice mechanisms also do not incur the social costs generated by worker turnover. One of the best documented effects of labor unions in the U.S. economy is the reduction of quit rates on the part of union members, due to a combination of higher union-negotiated wage rates and union grievance mechanisms.[8] Unions constitute an institutionalized memory for storing and retrieving information on workplace hazards that is absent in nonunion environments. Unions can enhance their members' understanding of job risks both by providing their own training and education sessions and by participating in management programs to ensure their effectiveness. As discussed in the Introduction and in chapter 3, labor unions have made the worker's right to know one of the central components of their health and safety programs.

Union policies and programs provide a useful antidote to the libertarian see-no-evil reliance upon market forces to achieve social goals. The notion that quit decisions represent uncoerced voluntary choices by individual workers has always been belied by the statistical association between individual quit decisions and macroeconomic conditions such as the rate of unemployment. Not surprisingly, quit rates rise during periods of full employment, when job options are plentiful, and decline during periods of high unemployment.[9] Far from being an autonomous expression of the worker's personal preferences, the quit decision is a socially conditioned response to labor market possibilities that are themselves influenced by economic policy at the national and international levels.

Union programs are also influenced by unemployment rates and macroeconomic conditions. Strikes and generous wage settlements are characteristic of economic upswings; recessions dampen strikes and produce more modest settlements. Nevertheless, union structures are far less sensitive to unemployment rates than are quit decisions by individual workers. Union contracts tend to be established for fixed periods of time, which insulates them somewhat from the ups and downs of the labor market. The day-in and day-out work of grievance mechanisms and safety committees grinds on with an internal logic of its own and breaks down only in the face of severe threats to job security.

Union activities restrain the sorting of disadvantaged workers into hazardous jobs that follows from the operation of labor markets. Union health and safety programs directly improve working conditions and provide an alternative to exit for highly skilled workers faced with hazards on the job. More important perhaps, the tendency of unions to raise wages produces the compensating differentials that laissez-faire economics has always ascribed to the invisible hand of labor market competition.[10] As documented in chapter 2, nonunion workers in hazardous jobs are much more likely to pursue union representation than are otherwise similar nonunion workers in safe jobs, and unions are more successful in winning representation rights there. Even if the unions that come to represent these workers do not actively focus on health and safety, they will raise wages and thereby provide indirect compensation and incentives for preventing hazards. This is only one manifestation of the well-documented tendency of labor union programs to benefit disproportionately those workers with the fewest options in the labor market.[11] Bargaining mechanisms produce outcomes that reflect the relative positions of the competing interests before the bargaining begins. Sitting together at the table allows workers to negotiate a different bargain than they would if seated individually.

Limits on the Voice Strategy:
Work Rules and the One-Party State

The voice strategy suffers from its own characteristic defects, however. As a method for signaling worker preferences concerning the appropriate mix of wages and working conditions, union programs amplify the views of one set of employees while muffling the views of another. Labor unions are democratic organizations run by elected officials whose personal self-interest lies in being reelected. As is the case in all democratic systems, some individual "citizens" carry more weight than others, due to their more active participation in politics. Union leadership must be particularly sensitive to organized caucuses within the membership.

The democratic nature of union politics has important implications for union strategies concerning workplace hazards. Where hazards are widespread and afflict a large portion of the membership, such as in mining or in some portions of the heavy manufacturing industry, health and safety may become a priority for the union. Where the hazards differ from job to job or are restricted to a minority of the membership, however, health and safety may be ignored. As is often pointed out by libertarian critics of democratic decision rules, political processes are less sensitive to the needs and preferences of each individual than are market mechanisms.

This distortion of individual preferences is partly endemic to any democratic system, but also partly a peculiarity of the industrial relations system developed in the United States since the passage of the National Labor Relations Act. The reliance upon collective bargaining and strike threats at the industrywide level requires union leaders to focus on those issues common to workers in many different firms and geographic areas. It is hardly surprising that they come to champion increases in wages and fringe benefits rather than improvements in working conditions, since these differ so much across work sites. With some exceptions, occupational health and safety has not served as a unifying theme for national negotiations between unions and management but has remained largely a local issue.

If the voice signal is distorted due to the democratic nature of most trade unions, it is also distorted due to the undemocratic nature of some. Labor unions in the United States have been plagued historically by corruption and dictatorial practices on the part of some union administrations, particularly in industries with small, dispersed firms and a relatively uneducated membership. Although they have received considerable media attention, these cases of dishonest authoritarianism are in fact isolated. Much more important are the cases of honest authoritarianism, where union leaders run their organizations in a legal fashion but without accepting the legitimacy of opposition from within the organization. The internal politics of large labor unions have been described as a one-party state.[12] This authoritarian structure is probably the rule rather than the exception in American labor unions at the national level, where the leadership is insulated from political opposition. At the local level, in contrast, union politics are usually quite democratic, and union leaders are regularly voted out of office.[13] This divergence between national and local union politics is in fact required by the industrial relations system, in which the national union must function on an almost military basis in order to confront successfully hierarchical corporations that themselves permit no democratic questioning of top management. Successful bargaining requires large industrywide, or at least firmwide, negotiations, which in turn require solidarity and discipline on the part of the membership. In this framework, dissent is easily interpreted as betrayal.

Labor unions impose their own set of efficiency costs on the economy, costs that must be weighed against the benefits of voice strategies for controlling occupational safety and health hazards. Most obviously, unionized work settings in the United States have negotiated complex rules governing many details of the work process. These work rules limit the ability of management to introduce cost-reducing new machinery or reallocate tasks within the work force. Attempts by management to tamper with these rules often produce intense conflict. While constraining some forms of industrial conflict, labor unions exacerbate shop floor conflict if necessary to maintain their hard-won work rules. As documented in chapter 4, strike rates are consistently higher in hazardous industries than in safe ones. To a large extent, the union focus on work rules is due to the fact that decision-making authority is concentrated in management's hands. With their skills limited to particular work sites, industrial workers have lost the mobility and easy employability of earlier craft workers and have come to depend on work rules for their job security.

Finally, trade unionism embodies some principles unattractive to much of the public. Collective bargaining assumes that the union-management bargaining process and its outcomes are fair. The citizenry at large is not always willing to accept collectively bargained outcomes, however, because they are seen to impose undesired costs on third parties or because they are considered unfair to particular workers. The National Labor Relations Act is remarkable, when viewed through contemporary eyes, in the way in which it accords rights to labor unions as institutions but not to labor union members as individuals. For example, it is the union and not the individual member who has the right to decide whether a problem can be pursued through the grievance and arbitration mechanism. There are good reasons for this allocation of rights, given the basic focus on collective action and the need to coordinate individual preferences in a unified bargaining position. The military analogy is again appropriate. Nevertheless, this focus runs against the grain of modern concepts of rights, which are increasingly skeptical of institutions and organizations of all types and are concerned for the status of the individual. If the process of collective bargaining is unfair to third parties or to particular workers, then the outcomes it produces are also considered unfair. This widespread public concern with externalities and individual rights has contributed in significant ways to the decline of labor unions and collective bargaining in the United States.

The Legal Strategy:
Judicial Protections against Force and Fraud

Workers have begun to pursue legal recourses as a response to the weaknesses of their exit and voice options. OSHA, state agencies, local fire departments, and emergency response systems now support the worker's right to know and the employer's duty to disclose hazard information. OSHA standards, environmental statutes, and state regulations support the worker's rights to refuse hazardous work and blow the whistle on socially unacceptable conditions. The courts are requiring firms who conceal hazards or produce unreasonably hazardous products to compensate the victims.

The right to know about hazards, the right to act in response, and the right to be compensated for harm suffered are consistent with exit and voice strategies, but they differ in seeking public guarantees of individual rights rather than relying solely upon the outcome of private bargaining mechanisms. These efforts are public in orientation, intervening in the day-to-day transactions of private markets to counter the effects of force and fraud. They are also individualistic in orientation, directly guaranteeing the rights of particular workers. This contrasts with the collective orientation of earlier public policy embodied in the National Labor Relations Act, which indirectly guaranteed the rights of individual workers by directly guaranteeing the rights of labor union organizations. It also contrasts with the social orientation of more recent public policy embodied in the Occupational Safety and Health Act, which focuses on the working environment rather than on the individual worker.

The principle underlying the legal strategy is that the agreements made by individuals and groups in the private economy are not necessarily fair, even if made voluntarily, because the rules governing market behavior are not necessarily fair. This contrasts with both the libertarian faith in individual choices and the trade unionist's faith in the balance of power. Market outcomes are subjected to external review by political and judicial institutions to ensure their compatibility with social principles of justice. This review mechanism assumes that private initiatives are valid only when fully informed and made in an uncoerced environment. It recognizes the susceptibility of market mechanisms to force and fraud and the essential role of governmental institutions in supporting markets.[14]

Limits on the Legal Strategy: Court Costs and the Fragmentation of Collective Protest

The legal strategy relies upon self-interested actions of individual workers, typically represented by a personal attorney, to achieve safer conditions or adequate compensation. This legal focus limits which issues are pursued, which workers pursue them, and which types of remediation are available. It can impede a clear recognition of the social nature of workplace problems by emphasizing individual rights over the public health.

Courtroom or administrative agency sanctions against employers for failure to warn about hazards, for discharge without just cause, or for negligent imposition of harm create incentives that may improve the functioning of labor markets. They do so by imposing compensatory and punitive damage awards, which often generate high attorney fees, lucrative payments to expert witnesses, and other court costs. There is no assurance that litigation will generate equal treatment for different individuals with equally pressing grievances. The outcomes of court cases depend heavily upon the peculiarities of individual attorneys, judges, and juries and not simply on the merits of each case. The unpredictability of outcomes gives defendants strong incentives to invest in legal expertise instead of safer working conditions.

Another major problem with the legal strategy is its tendency to focus on transgressions of rules rather than on the fairness of the rules themselves. In emphasizing the uniqueness of each case, the legal strategy can distract attention from the fact that many problems and many aspirations are common to all workers.[15] Unsafe working conditions and unfair personnel practices typically escape attention until an individual worker can prove he or she suffered financial losses subsequent to injury or discharge. The history of American industrial relations law is filled with efforts to fragment collective protests against the structure of the system into individual demands for restitution or compensation within the existing structure.[16]

A particularly important example of the deficiencies of public policies that focus exclusively on individual rights concerns the treatment of workers fired for seeking union representation. The discharge of prounion employees has emerged as one of the most common and effective tactics for defeating unionization efforts. These discharges are illegal, but employers have developed sophisticated methods for disguising their true motivations. Nevertheless, the number of employers found guilty of firing workers for prounion activity has grown dramatically. In 1980, for example, the number of workers officially recognized by the NLRB as fired for prounion activity equaled 5% of the total number of workers voting prounion in all elections. Given that most workers voting prounion are silent supporters of unionization, the risk of discharge during the preelection period for a vocally prounion worker is much higher than 5%.[17]

The basic right created by the NLRA is the workers' right "to self-organization, to form, join, or assist labor organizations, to bargain collectively through representatives of their choosing." It would seem logical for the NLRB to prevent employer interference with the employees' collective right of association. In practice, however, the NLRB has focused on repairing the harm inflicted by employers on individual workers rather than the harm inflicted on worker associations.[18] Workers illegally discharged for prounion activity are awarded back wages and, in some cases, reinstatement. If the employer's aim were to punish the discharged worker for prounion opinions, this remedy would fit the crime. But typically the employer's purpose is to defeat the union organizing effort. By the time the actively prounion employees are reinstated, the union's organizing momentum is often lost. Payment of lost wages to illegally discharged workers is much cheaper for employers than paying the higher wages negotiated by a union after a successful organizing effort. Reinstatement does not even compensate aggrieved individuals if the collective effort fails. Reinstated workers return to a hostile employer and rarely last long in the job. Only 40% of discharged workers awarded reinstatement actually return to their old jobs, and 80% of these have quit or been fired within two years. The main reason given by workers for quitting jobs after being reinstated is vindictive treatment by management.[19]

The Regulatory Strategy:
Exposure Limits and the Social Contract

Since 1970, government policy in occupational health has centered on the regulation of workplace exposures through the imposition of maximum permissible exposure limits. The growth in public support for regulation of environmental pollution has strengthened and been strengthened by the demand for controls on hazardous workplace exposures. Indeed, workplace exposures are often early warning signals of pollution and health problems that will later emerge in the environment and community at large.

Regulatory institutions such as OSHA enjoy great advantages over individual workers and labor unions in the interpretation and utilization of scientific information. The epidemiological and toxicological data pertaining to particular chemicals are highly technical and inherently difficult for nonspecialists to understand. Even in the best of imaginable circumstances, with a fully enforced Hazard Communication Standard and a strong and responsive labor union, workers are inherently disadvantaged. Furthermore, regulatory agencies usually have a better understanding than workers and unions of the engineering methods and economic costs of exposure limits.

Direct regulation of toxic substances avoids some of the economic costs associated with exit, voice, and legal strategies. It relies neither upon worker turnover nor upon industrial conflict to achieve its ends. Regulatory programs do not evaporate the moment the unemployment rate rises. They cover nonunion, as well as unionized, firms and are not vulnerable to the same manipulation of NLRB procedures that has undermined union organizing and collective bargaining. While OSHA standards are reviewed by the courts, they are not as subject to the idiosyncrasies of juries and theatrical skills of attorneys as are the legal strategies pursued by individual workers.

In contrast to exit and voice strategies, the regulatory strategy strives to ensure an acceptable outcome rather than merely establish an acceptable process. In contrast to the legal strategy, it focuses on achieving the best outcome for groups of workers rather than on compensating aggrieved individuals. This places the regulatory strategy within the tradition of the public health perspective, which from its origins has emphasized the creation of a healthy environment rather than of incentives for healthy behavior on the part of individuals. The regulatory strategy for controlling occupational safety and health hazards can be interpreted within the philosophical framework of the social contract.[20] This perspective adheres to the basic contractarian principle that the outcomes of a fair process are fair, but embodies a different understanding of what constitutes a fair process. Fair political principles are defined as ones that individuals would voluntarily agree to if they were ignorant of their particular skills and social positions. The social contract framework contrasts with the libertarian framework underlying the exit strategy and the industrial relations framework underlying the voice strategy, both of which permit the outcome of labor market contracts to depend on preexisting inequalities in wealth and ability.

All contractarian theories of justice place limits on the topics suitable for discussion and on the tactics that may be employed in the bargaining process. For example, no one is allowed to sell himself or herself into slavery on any terms, and no one is permitted to use force and fraud to compel consent by the opposing party. However, the various versions of contractarian theory differ with respect to the limitations they impose on the contracting process. Occupational health regulation presupposes fairly stringent limits on voluntary contracting, owing to a deeply held sentiment that health is more than just another marketplace good that individuals should be free to bargain away. Health is of value in its own right but is also a prerequisite for the enjoyment of many other possibilities. Inequalities in health status are less acceptable than inequalities in wealth. Libertarian critics of regulatory programs castigate this preference for health as arbitrary and paternalistic. They deny that any third party, such as a government regulatory agency, has the right to question the outcome of a process based on consent. Proponents of the regulatory strategy counter that the initial endowments and bargaining strategies available to particular individuals are so profoundly influenced by past injustices and morally arbitrary flukes of nature as to vitiate to a great extent the link between individual consent and social acceptability.

Limits on the Regulatory Strategy: Overregulation and Underregulation

While exit and voice signals struggle to be heard over the labor market cacophony, the regulatory mandate announces itself to the employer in the loud voice of the *Federal Register* and the compliance officer. Volume does not imply clarity, however, and the set of incentives provided by the regulatory system as a whole is ridden with inconsistencies. Some substances are regulated stringently while others escape OSHA's attention altogether. This juxtaposition of overregulation and underregulation is not coincidental; it is a characteristic feature of the system. The rhetoric of absolute safety that dominated OSHA's ideology during the 1970s impeded the coherent setting of priorities and smeared any compromise on exposure limits with the taint of immorality. This was clearly evident in the Generic Carcinogen Policy of 1980, discussed in chapter 9, which accorded equal regulatory treatment to substances with strong epidemiological evidence of cancer in humans and substances with only modest laboratory evidence of cancer in animals. During its heyday in the late 1970s, OSHA insisted on lowering the permissible exposure limit for every regulated substance to the lowest feasible level. This raised a maelstrom of political resistance, which translated itself into court rulings and executive orders requiring elaborate quantification of the expected economic costs and health benefits of every regulation. These bureaucratic requirements limited the number of substances that could be targeted for regulation, and virtually precluded successive rounds of regulation for any one substance. OSHA's embarrassing record of substance-specific carcinogen regulation was a direct and predictable outcome of a process that was oriented toward stringent control of a few hazards and complete neglect of others.[21] The political conflict produced by OSHA in its short history certainly rivals the turnover costs, industrial conflict, and burden of litigation generated by exit, voice, and legal responses to workplace hazards.

The overregulation of some substances and underregulation of others violate basic principles of cost-effectiveness, which maintain that policy efforts should be distributed across targets in such a way as to achieve the greatest overall impact. This ineffectiveness is compounded by the manner in which OSHA tends to regulate uniformly any substance that is used in more than one industry. OSHA has traditionally been reluctant to take into account differences across industries in the cost of compliance. Cost-effectiveness principles would insist that the agency impose strictest limits in those industries where compliance costs are lowest. OSHA's rhetorical absolutism prevents it from admitting that it permits any significant hazard to continue unabated, and therefore forces it to claim that the exposure limits feasible for the industries with the highest compliance costs are the best that need be demanded of industries with lower compliance costs. This was apparent in the creation of the Air Contaminants Standard discussed in chapter 9; in setting the standard OSHA adopted permissible exposure limits that were economically achievable in the most hazardous industries, and then tried to argue that the same limits would be safe for workers in all industries.

The philosophical objections to the regulatory strategy are obvious. Even granting the argument that agreements between employers and employees in the labor market are subject to considerable force and fraud, it is not clear that the solutions proposed by a regulatory institution such as OSHA are superior. The comparative advantage enjoyed by OSHA in understanding the scientific, engineering, and economic data relevant to risk management decisions is offset by its unfamiliarity with worker values and preferences. The geographical and cultural distance between OSHA's bureaucracy and America's shop floor always raises the specter of paternalistic social policy, whereby workers are viewed as so many passive recipients of governmental largess rather than as active protagonists who demand justice.

Substitutes or Complements?

Given the limitations inherent in each, none of the four basic strategies for controlling workplace hazards can be relied upon exclusively. Rather, as clearly evidenced over the past thirty years, workers and their allies pursue a mix of strategies, with the focus shifting from one option to another in response to changes in the larger economic and political environment. This raises the important question of how the four alternatives relate to one another. To what extent are they substitutes, duplicating or even undermining each other? To what extent are they complements, paralleling and strengthening each other?

The strongest argument that the alternative strategies are substitutes that should not be pursued simultaneously derives from economic models of labor market competition. Here, turnover costs from exit strategies impose the most effective incentives for investment in workplace protections. Voice and legal strategies reduce these incentives by strengthening workers' rights to act in their current jobs. The employment-at-will doctrine supports the exit alternative as the only employee strategy consistent with protection of employers' rights. Proponents of the exit strategy are vociferous in opposing government regulation of working conditions, on the grounds that this limits the ability of market mechanisms to establish the socially acceptable level and distribution of work-related illness.[22]

If the economic, political, and historical data presented in this book have proven anything, however, it is that this view of the labor market is inaccurate. Uncoordinated responses by individual workers in an unregulated labor market are often uninformed, inefficient, and influenced by social inequalities. Turnover costs do provide economic incentives for employers to improve working conditions, but only if the quits are based on reasonably accurate perceptions of the risks. The history of deception in the workplace convincingly demonstrates the need for voice and legal guarantees of the worker's right to know about workplace hazards.

It might also be argued that the voice and legal strategies are substitutes because they both protect the worker's right to know and right to act. The historical record does in fact show that legal guarantees of individual rights have spread during the same period that union representation has declined. This development of public guarantees has presumably been both a cause and a result of the decline in private guarantees. The historical record also shows, however, that labor unions have been at the forefront of political campaigns to obtain public guarantees of the right to know and the right to act. Unions have realized that their private efforts are strengthened by the presence of public statutes and standards that cover nonunion firms and that can be brought into play in unionized firms when the union's bargaining position is weak. Enthusiasts of the newly emerging public guarantees of workers' rights may be overinterpreting the efficacy of these developments in the absence of strong shop floor unionization.[23] The balance-of-power principle retains considerable validity in the contemporary labor market, and collective worker organizations such as labor unions are often essential for the successful pursuit of public rights by individual workers. Labor unions help workers file complaints of violations of OSHA's Hazard Communication Standard, NLRA and OSHA guarantees of the right to refuse hazardous work, and whistle-blower protections provided in many statutes. The increasingly prominent role played by labor-management health and safety committees in debates over how to provide public support for the worker's right to act illustrates the necessity for legal strategies to protect collective, as well as individual, initiatives.

Some critics of governmental regulation have heralded collective bargaining as a private sector substitute for public control.[24] Isolated union-negotiated improvements in exposure levels are used as evidence that OSHA is not needed and might impede creative private negotiations between employers and employees. In the context of the rapid erosion in union representation and bargaining power, this view is at best naive. Its role in the policy debate is to add fuel to the attacks on OSHA, which has proven capable of forcing significant development of safer production technologies in the face of massive employer resistance. The vitriolic denunciation of regulation and the disingenuous exaggeration of union power combine to make this perspective a variation on the libertarian's traditional theme: exit strategies within a juridical context of employment at will.

Early proponents of government regulation interpreted OSHA as a substitute for flawed strategies based on labor market incentives, collective bargaining, and court remedies.[25] Subsequent history has forced a reevaluation of this enthusiasm for command and control mechanisms. Regulatory strategies depend upon grass-roots mobilization both for political support against industry lobbying in Washington and for shop floor monitoring of industry compliance with existing standards. OSHA's efforts to strengthen the worker's right to know and right to act are integral parts of its strategy to impose and enforce permissible exposure limits. Conversely, hazard disclosure and worker mobilization efforts benefit from the standards-setting process, which evaluates health risks and the economic feasibility of control technologies in a systematic fashion that is beyond the capabilities of individual workers and labor unions.

Conclusion

Society has three fundamental goals in occupational health policy. Efficiency is pursued through incentives for the development of new products and processes that minimize health and safety hazards while upholding a dynamic market economy. Responsiveness to individual values and preferences is pursued through marketplace, workplace, legal, and political systems that are conducive to both individual liberty and collective democracy. Fairness is pursued through a structure of social institutions that limit the tendency of private agreements to impose costs on third parties and take advantage of unequal bargaining positions.

Efficiency in the pursuit of occupational health goals is important because the resources used in this arena could be used elsewhere, improving health through other means or achieving nonhealth objectives. The inevitability of limited resources highlights the importance of efficiency and cost-effectiveness in the pursuit of each particular strategy and in the choice among alternative strategies. Efforts need to be targeted to achieve the greatest possible improvement in working conditions while imposing the least possible burden on the economy.

Efficiency alone, however, is radically inadequate as a criterion for evaluating occupational health strategies. Efficiency is instrumental only, eloquent as to the means but silent as to the ends of social policy. The ends are to be sought elsewhere, in the outcome of political processes that respond to the preferences of the citizenry. Safety and health on the job is only one of many concerns important to workers. Social policy in a liberal and democratic system derives its priorities from the priorities of its individual members. Although public health professionals emphasize the reduction of exposures to the lowest technologically feasible level, other social goals legitimately compete for our attention. There exists no set of objectively necessary ends that must be pursued regardless of the values and desires of individuals. This emphasis on subjective values does not entail, however, any policy subservience to ill-considered individual preferences. Only reflective preferences are strong enough to bear the responsibility for directing social policies. Education and self-education are central functions of all individuals, groups, and societies. The educational process is not only an instrumental one of discovering new means for achieving established ends, but involves the discovery and creation of genuinely new ends.

Responsiveness to reflective preferences is also inadequate, however, as a foundation for occupational health policy. Individuals' preferences often conflict, even after extensive discussion and debate that dispel misunderstandings and clarify the important issues at stake. Some social mechanism must be established to adjudicate conflicting claims. The existing level and distribution of work-related injury and illness reflect the existing inequalities in economic wealth and political power. Unless one accepts the notion that "might makes right," an independent principle is needed for evaluating conflicting preferences and balancing competing interests. In a liberal society, the basic principle for adjudicating claims must be the principle of fairness. Wherever possible, political institutions must respect the arrangements agreed to by private parties, because these are most likely to be voluntary. Where private agreements are subject to considerable force and fraud, however, political institutions have an obligation to intervene. The criterion for evaluating existing outcomes, including health and safety in the workplace, is how they compare to the outcomes that would have been produced by truly voluntary agreements that were not subject to force and fraud.

The exit, voice, legal, and regulatory strategies together provide efficient and effective means for controlling occupational safety and health hazards. In their own ways they reflect social preferences and facilitate the fair resolution of labor-management conflicts. Workers and their allies rely on the combined strengths of the four strategies to achieve safety and justice in the workplace.

Notes

Introduction

1. A number of articles and one book have covered the DBCP issue: D. Weir and C. Matthiessen, "Will the Circle Be Unbroken?" *Mother Jones*, June 1989; E. Yonay, "The Nematode Chronicles," *New West*, May 1981; R. Taylor, "DBCP Still Used Despite Dangers," *Los Angeles Times*, 28 June 1979; D. Ben-Horin, "The Sterility Scandal," *Mother Jones*, May 1979; "Dow and Shell Bow Out of DBCP," *Chemical Week*, 5 April 1978; C. Trost, *Elements of Risk* (New York, 1984). The information on union activities at Occidental Chemical is largely drawn from a lengthy letter of 26 June 1979 to the editor of *Mother Jones* written by R. Moure, industrial hygienist for the Oil, Chemical, and Atomic Workers.

Chapter 2

1. W. K. Viscusi, "Job Hazards and Worker Quit Rates: An Analysis of Adaptive Worker Behavior," *International Economic Review*, 1979, 20(1):29–58; W. K. Viscusi and C. O'Connor, "Adaptive Responses to Chemical Labelling: Are Workers Bayesian Decision Makers?" *American Economic Review*, 1984, 74(5):942–56.

2. W. K. Viscusi, *Risk by Choice* (Cambridge, Mass., 1983); *Economic Report of the President* (Washington, January 1987), 179–208.

3. Further information on the calculation of these rates can be found in J. C. Robinson, "Exposure to Occupational Hazards among Hispanics, Blacks, and Non-Hispanic Whites in California," *American Journal of Public Health*, 1989, 79 (5):629–30.

4. QES respondents were considered to perceive their jobs as hazardous if any of thirteen categories of exposures posed a "sizeable problem" or "great problem." These categories were (1) "dangerous chemicals"; (2) "dangers from fire, burn, or shock"; (3) "air pollution from dust, smoke, gas, fumes, fibers, or other things"; (4) "working outside in bad weather"; (5) "extremes of temperature or humidity indoors"; (6) "dirty or badly maintained areas in [the] workplace"; (7) "things that are placed or stored dangerously"; (8) "too much noise"; (9) "dangerous tools, machinery, or equipment"; (10) "risk of catching disease"; (11) "risk of traffic accidents while working"; (12) "risk of personal attack by people or animals"; and (13) "dangerous work methods."

5. NLS respondents were designated as perceiving their jobs as hazardous if they gave a score of three or four in response to either "the job is dangerous" or "you are exposed to unhealthy conditions." The surveys were set up on a scale of one to four, with one meaning "not true at all" and four meaning "very true."

6. AFL respondents were designated as perceiving their jobs as hazardous if they reported being concerned "a great deal" or "only somewhat" with "exposure to health and safety dangers."

7. U.S. Bureau of Labor Statistics, *Handbook of Labor Statistics*, Bulletin 2340 (Washington, August 1989), table 142.

8. The RTECS data base contains information on a variety of toxicological effects of chemical substances, including positive findings that the substances are carcinogenic, neoplastic (causing tumors that neither invade tissues nor metastasize), teratogenic (causing birth defects), mutagenic (causing chromosomal changes), or irritants to the skin or eyes. The index used here is limited to chemicals with positive find-

ings on carcinogenicity. The NIOSH methodology is described in D. H. Pedersen, R. O. Young, and D. S. Sundin, *A Model for the Identification of High Risk Occupational Groups Using RTECS and NOHS Data*, U.S. Department of Health and Human Services, National Institute for Occupational Safety and Health (Cincinnati, 1983).

9. In response to a request from the author, NIOSH created a risk index for each of the 231 three-digit census occupations for which data were available. This index is based on dose information; chemicals producing carcinogenic effects at lower doses are weighted more heavily in the index than chemicals whose minimum doses for carcinogenic effects are higher. Exposures reported by the engineers as "controlled" are weighted by a factor of 0.1; exposures reported as part-time are weighted by a factor of 0.5. This manner of index construction is in accord with the general algorithm for index construction developed by NIOSH.

10. The 1984 AFL survey is not used here, since it only codes the respondent's occupation at the broad one-digit level. The QES and NLS data can be matched with the cancer risk index at the detailed three-digit occupation level. Again in contrast to the QES and NLS, the AFL does not query respondents concerning exposure to health hazards separately from safety hazards.

11. For a more detailed presentation and discussion of these findings, see J. C. Robinson, "Worker Responses to Occupational Risk of Cancer," *Review of Economics and Statistics*, 1990, 72(3):536–71.

12. W. K. Viscusi, *Employment Hazards: An Investigation of Market Performance* (Cambridge, Mass., 1979).

13. QES respondents were designated as intending to quit if they said they were "very likely" or "somewhat likely" to "make a genuine effort to find a new job with another employer within the next year." AFL respondents were asked: "Do you plan to stay at your present job for the next year or two, or do you plan to change jobs?" They were designated as intending to quit if they said they "plan to change jobs."

14. For a more complete statistical analysis of hazards and quits, see J. C. Robinson, "Worker Responses to Workplace Hazards," *Journal of Health Politics, Policy, and Law*, 1987, 12(4):665–82.

15. P. Weiler, "Striking a New Balance: Freedom of Contract and the Prospects for Union Representation," *Harvard Law Review*, 1984, 98(2):351–99; W. Cooke, *Union Organizing and Public Policy: The Failure to Secure First Contracts* (Kalamazoo, Mich., 1985).

16. The analysis of the QES and NLS data is discussed in more depth in J. C. Robinson, "Workplace Hazards and Worker Desires for Union Representation," *Journal of Labor Research*, 1988, 9(3):237–39.

17. The full list of independent variables included the industry injury rate, percentage of the industry work force that was unionized, characteristics of the nonunion workers in the industry (percentage black, percentage female, percentage with less than twelve years of education), the difference in average industry wages for union and nonunion workers, the number eligible to vote, the square of the number eligible, the percentage who voted, whether the first election was conclusive, whether the employer consented to the election, the logarithm of the number of months of election campaign, five unit type categories (craft, departmental, transport operatives, industrial, other), whether the union was the Teamsters, whether the union was AFL-CIO affiliated, and whether two or more unions participated.

18. These data are treated in more detail in J. C. Robinson, "Labor Union Involvement in Occupational Safety and Health, 1957–1987," *Journal of Health Politics, Policy, and Law*, 1988, 13(3):453–68.

Chapter 3

1. For a discussion of the NLRB's positions and for a full set of references to the legal literature, see M. Mentzer, "Unions' Right to Information about Occupational Health

Hazards under the National Labor Relations Act," *Industrial Relations Law Journal,* 1983, 5:247–82.

2. Bureau of National Affairs, *Occupational Safety and Health Reporter,* 22 April 1982, 979. Also see the discussion in Mentzer, "Unions' Right to Information," 247–82.

3. For further discussion of these and related health and safety programs at the UAW, see United Auto Workers, *Solidarity,* May 1985. Also see F. E. Mirer, "Worker Participation in Health and Safety: Lessons from Joint Programs in the American Automobile Industry," *American Industrial Hygiene Association Journal,* 1989, 50:598–603.

4. P. Brodeur, *Expendable Americans* (New York, 1974); id. *Outrageous Misconduct: The Asbestos Industry on Trial* (New York, 1985); B. Castleman, *Asbestos: Medical and Legal Aspects* (Clifton, N.J. 1986).

5. R. Bayer, "Notifying Workers at Risk: The Politics of the Right-to-Know," *American Journal of Public Health,* 1986, 76:1352–56; P. A. Schulte and K. Ringen, "Notification of Workers at High Risk: An Emerging Public Health Problem," *American Journal of Public Health,* 1984, 74(5):485–91.

6. M. Silverstein, N. Maizlish, R. Park, and F. Mirer, "Mortality among Workers Exposed to Coal Tar Pitch Volatiles and Welding Emissions: An Exercise in Epidemiologic Triage," *American Journal of Public Health,* 1985, 75(11):1283–87.

7. For more detailed analyses of the relationship between right to refuse hazardous work protections under public law and private collective bargaining, see N. A. Ashford and J. Katz, "Unsafe Working Conditions: Employee Rights Under the Labor Management Relations Act and the Occupational Safety and Health Act," *Notre Dame Lawyer,* 1977, 52:802–36; see also L. Drapkin, "The Right to Refuse Hazardous Work after Whirlpool," *Industrial Relations Law Journal,* 1980, 4:29–60.

8. Trends in the prevalence of hazardous work refusal clauses in union contracts are discussed in the next section. Examples of such clauses can be found in P. Chown, *Workplace*

Health and Safety: A Guide to Collective Bargaining (Berkeley, 1980).

9. J. Gross and P. Greenfield, "Arbitral Value Judgments in Health and Safety Disputes: Management Rights Over Workers' Rights," *Buffalo Law Review*, 1985, 34:546–691.

10. A. Derickson, *Workers' Health, Workers' Democracy: The Western Miners' Struggle, 1891–1925* (Ithaca, N.Y., 1988).

11. Bureau of National Affairs, *Basic Patterns in Union Contracts*, selected editions (Washington, 1957–1987).

12. U.S. Bureau of Labor Statistics, *Characteristics of Major Collective Bargaining Agreements*, selected editions (Washington, 1970–1980).

13. U.S. Bureau of Labor Statistics, *Labor Management Contract Provisions, 1949–1950*, Bulletin 1022 (Washington, 1951).

14. California Department of Industrial Relations, *Provisions for Union-Management Safety Committees in California Union Agreements* (San Francisco, February 1952).

15. L. Bacow, *Bargaining for Job Safety and Health* (Cambridge, Mass., 1980).

16. R. H. Sims, *Hazard Abatement as a Function of Firm Size: The Effects of Internal Firm Characteristics and External Incentives* (Ann Arbor, Mich., 1989).

17. U.S. Bureau of Labor Statistics, *Major Collective Bargaining Agreements: Safety and Health Provisions*, Bulletin 1425-16 (Washington, 1976).

18. Chown, *Workplace Health and Safety.*

19. U.S. Bureau of Labor Statistics, *Major Collective Bargaining Agreements*, Bulletin 1425-16.

20. U.S. Bureau of Labor Statistics, *Collective Bargaining Clauses: Labor-Management Safety, Production, and Industry Stabilization Committees*, Bulletin 1201 (Washington, 1956).

21. T. Kochan, L. Dyer, and D. Lipsky, *The Effectiveness of Union-Management Safety and Health Committees* (Kalamazoo, Mich., 1977).

22. American Center for the Quality of Work Life, "A Few Highlights from the Preliminary Findings of a National Occu-

pational Safety and Health Survey Conducted by the American Center for the Quality of Work Life in April 1984," cited on page 43 of the Department of Labor bulletin referred to in note 23.

23. U.S. Department of Labor, Bureau of Labor-Management Relations and Cooperative Programs, *The Role of Labor-Management Committees in Safeguarding Worker Safety and Health*, BLMR 121 (Washington, 1989).

24. Ibid.

Chapter 4

1. The QES and AFL posed the following question: "All in all, how satisfied would you say you are with your job—very satisfied, somewhat satisfied, not too satisfied, or not at all satisfied?" Workers were designated as dissatisfied in this analysis if they responded "not too satisfied" or "not at all satisfied"; otherwise they were designated as satisfied. The NLS posed the following question: "How do you feel about the job you have now? Do you: (1) Like it very much? (2) Like it fairly well? (3) Dislike it somewhat? (4) Dislike it very much?" Workers were designated as dissatisfied in this analysis if they responded "dislike it somewhat" or "dislike it very much."

2. The positive association between workplace hazards and worker dissatisfaction is also found using "objective," as distinct from worker-reported measures of hazard. A full discussion of these results can be found in Robinson, "Worker Responses to Workplace Hazards," 665–82.

3. S. Allen, "Compensation, Safety, and Absenteeism: Evidence from the Paper Industry," *Industrial and Labor Relations Review*, 1981, 34(2):207–18.

4. S. Allen, "An Empirical Model of Work Attendance," *Review of Economics and Statistics*, 1981, 68(1):77–87.

5. The adjusted discharge rates control for average hourly earnings; percentage unionized; mean years of work force education, age, and job tenure; percentage of the work force that is female, black, residing in an SMSA, and residing in each

region of the nation. A full discussion of these data may be found in Robinson, "Worker Responses to Workplace Hazards," 665–82.

6. Since nonunion workers rarely go on strike, the strike analyses are limited to unionized PSID workers.

7. For a detailed treatment of these data, see Robinson, "Worker Responses to Workplace Hazards," 665–82. The 1985–87 PSID analyzes control for log hourly wages, sex, race, tenure, age, age squared, five educational level categories, plus region and city size variables. The sample size was 858.

8. J. Leigh, "Risk Preference and the Interindustry Propensity to Strike," *Industrial and Labor Relations Review*, 1983, 36(2):271–85.

9. D. Byrne and R. King, "Wildcat Strikes in U.S. Manufacturing, 1960–1977," *Journal of Labor Research*, 1986, 7(4): 387–402.

10. S. Flaherty, "Strike Activity, Worker Militancy, and Productivity Change in Manufacturing, 1961–1981," *Industrial and Labor Relations Review*, 1987, 40(4):585–600.

11. J. R. Norsworthy and C. Zabala, "Worker Attitudes, Worker Behavior, and Productivity in the U.S. Automobile Industry, 1959–1976," *Industrial and Labor Relations Review*, 1985, 38(4):544–57.

12. H. Katz, T. Kochan, and K. Gobeille, "Industrial Relations Performance, Economic Performance, and QWL Programs: An Interplant Analysis," *Industrial and Labor Relations Review*, 1983, 37(1):3–17.

13. C. Ichniowski, *Fuzzy Frontiers of Production: Evidence of Persistent Inefficiency in Safety Expenditures*, National Bureau of Economic Research, Working Paper 1366 (Cambridge, Mass., June 1984).

14. These data were made available by Professor Wayne Gray of Clark University. Further information on the data can be obtained from W. Gray, "The Cost of Regulation: OSHA, EPA, and the Productivity Slowdown," *American Economic Review*, 1987, 77(5):998–1006.

15. In some instances, injury rates are published only on the three-digit level. For these industries and years, all four-

digit industries were assigned the injury rate for their three-digit industry. Injury rates for years prior to 1971 were recalibrated from cases per million hours worked to cases per hundred workers per year to make them comparable with the later data. Hazardous industries were defined as those with a logarithmic injury rate one standard deviation above the sample mean, and conversely for safe industries. The level of productivity in hazardous industries in a particular year was computed as the exponent of $[Q + (SD \times B)]$ where Q is the sample average of log output per hour, SD is the standard deviation of the log injury rate, and B is the least squares parameter estimate on the log injury rate in the translog production function. In order to ensure comparability in the definition of hazardous and safe industries across years, SD is measured as the sample average of the five log standard deviations for 1959, 1963, 1968, 1973, and 1978.

16. This is a statistically insignificant difference. All the other differences between hazardous and safe industries in table 16 are statistically significant.

17. This return on capital measure was developed in W. T. Dickens and L. F. Katz, "Inter-industry Wage Differences and Industry Characteristics," in *Unemployment and the Structure of Labor Markets*, ed. K. Lang and J. S. Leonard (New York, 1987).

18. The structure of each industry is measured by the percentage of total industry output accounted for by the four largest firms (four-firm concentration ratio). Ease of entry is inherently difficult to measure. Consistent with other studies of profitability, this analysis uses average firm size, advertising expenditures as a percentage of value of shipments, and value of assets as a percentage of value of shipments. Union strength is measured in terms of the percentage of the total work force represented by unions. Changes in consumer demand are measured using the 1972 to 1977 percentage rate of change in value of shipments, adjusted for price inflation.

19. These differences are statistically significant at the 99% confidence level.

20. Industries are classified as concentrated if the four-firm concentration ratio exceeded the sample median of 35, and otherwise as unconcentrated. The distribution of industries according to their injury rates is quite similar in the competitive and concentrated sectors, with a mean of 5.7 in the competitive sector and 5.3 in the concentrated sector. The dispersion of injury rates is narrower in the concentrated sector than in the competitive sector, however, with a standard deviation of 2.5, compared to 3.3. The standard deviation of the injury rate for all 398 manufacturing industries is 2.9.

21. The percentage unionized exerts no significant influence on profitability in the competitive sector, and so the association between injury rates and profitability in that sector does not vary according to whether one adjusts for unionization or not.

Chapter 5

1. A. Smith, *The Wealth of Nations* (1776; Baltimore, 1974), 201.

2. J. S. Mill, *The Principles of Political Economy*, vol. 2 of *The Collected Works* (1848; Toronto, 1965), 474–75.

3. This provides an additional possible explanation for the lower labor productivity in hazardous as compared to safe manufacturing industries that was documented in chapter 4. Skill differences alone, however, cannot explain the other dimensions of industrial conflict reported in that chapter, such as dissatisfaction, absenteeism, strikes, and profits.

4. A more detailed discussion of the methodology used in this section can be found in J. C. Robinson, "Hazardous Occupations within the Job Hierarchy," *Industrial Relations*, 1988, 27(2):241–50.

5. N. Root and D. Sebastian, "BLS Develops Measure of Job Risk by Occupation," *Monthly Labor Review*, 1981, 104:26–30.

6. Jobs are considered to offer poor training and promotion possibilities for QES workers if the workers "disagree" or "strongly disagree" with the following statements: "My job

requires that I keep learning new things" and "The chances for promotion are good." For NLS workers, jobs are considered to offer poor training and promotion possibilities if workers give a score of one or two in response to these statements: "The skills you are learning would be valuable in getting a better job" and "The chances for promotion are good." Here a score of one means "not true at all," a score of four means "very true," and scores of two and three are not explicitly defined.

7. These questions are not posed in the NLS or other available surveys.

8. Jobs are designated as uncreative and monotonous if the QES interviewees "disagree" or "strongly disagree" with the following statements: "My job requires that I be creative" and "I get to do a number of different things on my job." Jobs are designated as meaningless if the workers "agree" or "strongly agree" with this statement: "I feel that most of the things I do on my job are meaningless."

9. Workers are designated as having no control over job duties if they reply "somewhat hard" or "very hard" to the following: "Suppose there were some particular duties on your job that you wanted changed. How hard would it be to get them changed?" Workers are designated as having no control over the pace and hours of work, respectively, if they "disagree" or "strongly disagree" with these statements: "I determine the pace at which I work" and "The hours are good." Workers are designated as subject to rules and regulations if they "agree" or "strongly agree" with the statement quoted in the text.

10. Industries in the BLS data set were defined as hazardous or safe based on the occupational mix of the industry work force; the Workers' Compensation-based risk index for each industry was calculated as the employment-weighted risk index for each occupational group in the industry.

11. QES workers were asked: "Do you think of your job as one where you have regular, steady work throughout the year, is it seasonal, are there frequent layoffs, or what?" The job is

designated as insecure in this analysis if the worker reports a "sizeable problem" or "great problem" because the work is "seasonal" or subject to "frequent layoffs" or if the worker "works when there is work." NLS workers were designated as employed in insecure jobs if they gave a score of one or two to this statement: "The job security is good"; a score of one means "not true at all," a score of four means "very true," and scores of two and three are not defined.

12. QES workers are designated as expecting permanent layoff if they reply "somewhat likely" or "very likely" to the following: "Sometimes people permanently lose jobs they want to keep. How likely is it that during the next couple of years you will lose your present job and have to look for a job with another employer?"

13. The average monthly rate of recalls, multiplied by 12, was used as the annual rate of temporary layoffs. The annual rate of permanent layoffs was calculated as 12 times the average monthly layoff rate, minus the annual rate of temporary layoffs.

14. The layoff rates are higher in the NLS than in the PSID and BLS data since the NLS figures span two years.

15. A more detailed analysis and discussion of these data may be found in J. C. Robinson, "Job Hazards and Job Security," *Journal of Health Politics, Policy, and Law*, 1986, 11(1):1–17. The analysis underlying table 21 used the Workers' Compensation-based measure of relative risk by occupation rather than the industry injury rate used in the earlier paper. The 1985 PSID figures are calculated for 3,624 workers employed in 1985, 6.5% of which permanently lost their jobs over the next two years.

16. The statistical approach adopted here is similar to that reported in detail in J. C. Robinson, "Hazard Pay in Unsafe Jobs: Theory, Evidence, and Policy Implications," *Milbank Quarterly*, 1986, 64(4):650–77.

17. For surveys of the empirical studies of compensating wage differentials, see R. Smith, "Compensating Differentials and Public Policy," *Industrial and Labor Relations Review*,

1979, 23(3):339–52; C. Brown, "Compensating Differentials in the Labor Market," *Quarterly Journal of Economics*, 1980, 94(1):113–34; A. Fisher, L. G. Chestnut, and D. M. Violette, "The Value of Reducing Risks of Death: A Note on New Evidence," *Journal of Policy Analysis and Management*, 1989, 8(1):88–100.

Chapter 6

1. Further information on the data and methods used in developing these injury and illness rates can be found in Robinson, "Exposure to Occupational Hazards," 629–30.

2. For more information on occupational injury and illness rates in California, see J. C. Robinson, "The Rising Long-Term Trend in Occupational Injury Rates," *American Journal of Public Health*, 1988, 78:276–81. Also consult annual issues of California Department of Industrial Relations, Division of Labor Statistics and Research, *California Work Injuries and Illnesses* (San Francisco).

3. P. Berstein, *Discrimination, Jobs, and Politics: The Struggle for Equal Employment Opportunity in the United States Since the New Deal* (Chicago, 1985).

4. R. E. B. Lucas, "The Distribution of Job Characteristics," *Review of Economics and Statistics*, 1974, 56:530–40.

5. The CPS and PSID do not contain direct information on occupational injuries. The injury rates were obtained at the industry level from published sources and linked to the worker data using industry codes contained in the surveys. Thus each worker is ascribed the risk of injury equal to the average rate of injuries for all workers in his or her industry for the year. These industry injury rates were then weighted to account for the substantial differences in injury rates across occupations within particular industries. The industry-specific occupational risk weights were developed by the U.S. Bureau of Labor Statistics using Workers' Compensation data for broad (one-digit) occupational classifications. Details on the methods used in these analyses can be found in J. C. Robinson, "Trends in Racial Inequality and Exposure to Work-

Related Hazards," *Milbank Quarterly*, 1987, 65 (Supplement 2):404–20.

6. *Economic Report of the President* (Washington, January 1987), table B-38.

7. C. Brown, "Black-White Earnings Ratios Since the Civil Rights Act of 1964: The Importance of Labor Market Dropouts," *Quarterly Journal of Economics*, 1984, 99:31–44.

8. R. B. Freeman and J. L. Medoff, *What Do Unions Do?* (New York, 1984).

Chapter 7

1. M. Cherniak, *The Hawk's Nest Incident: America's Worst Industrial Disaster* (New Haven, 1986).

2. W. S. Randall and S. D. Solomon, *Building Six: The Tragedy at Bridesburg* (Boston, 1977).

3. C. D. Stone, "A Slap on the Wrist for the Kepone Mob," *Business and Society Review*, 1977, 22:4–11.

4. A. Derickson, "On the Dump Heap: Employee Medical Screening in the Tri-State Zinc-Lead Industry, 1924–1932," *Business History Review*, 1988, 62:656–77.

5. Castleman, *Asbestos*; Brodeur, *Outrageous Misconduct*; id., *Expendable Americans*; D. Kotelchuck, "Asbestos Research: Winning the Battle but Losing the War," *Health PAC Bulletin*, 1974, 61:1–32; M. Handelman and D. Kotelchuck, "Your Job or Your Life," *Health PAC Bulletin*, 1973, 50:1–15.

6. Occupational Safety and Health Administration, "Notice of Proposed Rulemaking: Hazard Identification; Notice of Public Rulemaking and Public Hearings." 46 *Federal Register* 4412 (1981); Bureau of National Affairs, *Occupational Safety and Health Reporter*, 22 January 1981, 835–36.

7. Bureau of National Affairs, *Occupational Safety and Health Reporter*, 19 February 1981, 1265.

8. Ibid., 26 March 1981, 1365.

9. Ibid., 14 April 1983, 960.

10. Occupational Safety and Health Administration, "Proposed Modification, Access to Employee Exposure and Medical Records," 47 *Federal Register* 30426 (1982).

11. Bureau of National Affairs, *Occupational Safety and Health Reporter*, 26 November 1981, 495.

12. Ibid., 15 July 1982, 147–48.

13. Ibid., 2 April 1981, 1388–89.

14. Ibid., 23 April 1981, 1478.

15. R. Howard, "There is Life After Auchter—At Least in Philadelphia," *In These Times*, 16–22 September 1981.

16. Bureau of National Affairs, *Chemical Right-to-Know Requirements: Federal and State Laws and Regulations, A Status Report* (Washington, 1984).

17. Ibid., 20–21.

18. Bureau of National Affairs, *Occupational Safety and Health Reporter*, 13 June 1985, 27.

19. Ibid., 27 February 1986, 996–97.

20. Ibid., 20 February 1986, 979.

21. Ibid., 17 December 1986, 800–801.

22. Ibid., 29 July 1987, 295.

23. Ibid., 23 August 1984, 259–60.

24. Ibid., 4 May 1988, 1770.

25. J. Lublin, "Chemical Firms Hope Reagan Will Keep Some Regulations," *Wall Street Journal*, 1 February 1982.

26. N. A. Ashford, *Crisis in the Workplace* (Cambridge, Mass., 1976).

27. Occupational Health and Safety Administration, "Final Rule: Hazard Communication." 48 *Federal Register* 53280 (1983).

28. Petitioner's reply brief, Public Citizen et al. v. Thorne Auchter, United States Court of Appeals for the Third Circuit (No. 83-3565), 30 August 1984, p. 4, addenda 1 and 2.

29. Bureau of National Affairs, *Occupational Safety and Health Reporter*, 10 June 1982, 30–31.

30. A. Oleinick, W. J. Fodor, and M. M. Susselman, "Risk Management for Hazardous Chemicals: OSHA's Hazard Communication Standard and EPA's Emergency Planning and Community Right-to-Know Regulations," *Journal of Legal Medicine*, 1988, 9(2):179–278.

31. Bureau of National Affairs, *Occupational Safety and Health Reporter*, 10 June 1982, 30–31.

32. J. Shepard, *Working in the Dark: Reagan and the "Right to Know" about Occupational Hazards* (Washington, 1986), 20–26.

33. Bureau of National Affairs, *Occupational Safety and Health Reporter*, 14 June 1984, 19–20.

34. Ibid., 30 May 1985, 1020–21.

35. Ibid., 25 March 1987, 1109.

36. Ibid., 19 August 1987, 483.

37. Occupational Health and Safety Administration, "Final Rule: Hazard Communication." 52 *Federal Register* 31852 (1987).

38. A. B. Morrison, "OMB Interference with Agency Rulemaking: The Wrong Way to Write a Regulation," *Harvard Law Review*, 1986, 99:1059–74.

39. Bureau of National Affairs, *Occupational Safety and Health Reporter*, 27 January 1988, 1331–32.

40. Ibid., 6 April 1988, 1614.

41. Ibid., 4 January 1989, 1419.

42. Ibid., 1 March 1989, 1671–72.

43. Ibid., 28 February 1990, 1747–48.

44. S. A. Treat, "The New Jersey Right to Know Act," *Rutgers Law Review*, 1986, 38:755–90.

45. Bureau of National Affairs, *Occupational Safety and Health Reporter*, 10 January 1985, 579–80.

46. Ibid., 17 October 1985, 403–4.

47. Ibid., 18 October 1984, 399–400.

48. Ibid., 2 January 1986, 845–46.

49. Ibid., 17 September 1986, 403.

50. Ibid., 24 September 1986, 423–24.

51. S. Jananoff, "The Bhopal Disaster and the Right to Know," *Social Science and Medicine*, 1988, 27(10):1113–23.

52. Oleinick, Fodor, and Susselman, "Risk Management for Hazardous Chemicals," 179–278.

53. J. R. Burcat and A. K. Hoffman, "The Emergency Planning and Community Right-to-know Act of 1986: An Explanation of Title III of SARA," *Environmental Law Reporter*, 1988, 18:10007–27; M. E. Kriz, *Chemicals and the Community: New*

Law, New Responsibilities (Washington, 1987); S. G. Hadden, *A Citizen's Right to Know: Risk Communication and Public Policy* (Boulder, Colo., 1989).

Chapter 8

1. C. C. Heckscher, *The New Unionism* (New York, 1988).

2. K. E. Klare, "The Public/Private Distinction in Labor Law," *University of Pennsylvania Law Review*, 1982, 130:1358–1422.

3. There exists a vast legal literature on the employment-at-will doctrine. For an introduction to this literature, with references for further reading, see Note, "Protecting Employees at Will against Wrongful Discharge: The Public Policy Exception," *Harvard Law Review*, 1983, 96:1931–51. For an argument in support of the at-will doctrine, see R. A. Epstein, "In Defense of the Contract at Will," *University of Chicago Law Review*, 1984, 51:946–87.

4. For a comparison of at-will employment practices with unionized systems ruled by outside arbitration, see C. W. Summers, "Individual Protections against Unjust Dismissal: Time for a Statute," *Virginia Law Review*, 1976, 62:481–532.

5. Mentzer, "Unions' Right to Information," 247–82.

6. T. A. Kochan, H. C. Katz, and R. B. McKersie, *The Transformation of American Industrial Relations* (New York, 1986).

7. D. W. Ewing, *Justice on the Job: Resolving Grievances in the Nonunion Workplace* (Boston, 1989).

8. T. A. Kochan, R. B. McKersie, and J. Chalykoff, "The Effects of Corporate Strategy and Workplace Innovations on Union Representation," *Industrial and Labor Relations Review*, 1986, 39(4):487–501; J. Firito, C. Lowman, and F. D. Nelson, "The Impact of Human Resource Policies on Union Organizing," *Industrial Relations*, 1987, 26(2):113–26.

9. W. T. Dickens, D. R. Wholey, and J. C. Robinson, "Correlates of Union Support in NLRB Elections," *Industrial Relations*, 1987, 26(3):240–52. The 1983 election-level statistical analyses discussed in chapter 3 also found a strong inverse re-

lationship between the size of the bargaining unit and the probability of union success.

10. Heckscher, *New Unionism*.

11. Kochan, Katz, and McKersie, *Transformation of American Industrial Relations*.

12. T. A. Kochan, H. C. Katz, and N. R. Mower, *Worker Participation and American Unions: Threat or Opportunity?* (Kalamazoo, Mich., 1984).

13. W. N. Outten and N. A. Kinigstein, *The Rights of Employees: The Basic ACLU Guide to an Employee's Rights* (New York, 1984).

14. Payne v. Western & ARR, 81 Tenn. 507 (1884).

15. Note, "The Public Policy Exception," 1931–51; D. T. Schibley, "The Employment-at-Will Doctrine: Providing a Public Policy Exception to Improve Worker Safety," *University of Michigan Journal of Law Reform*, 1983, 16(2):435–48.

16. Occupational Safety and Health Act of 1970, 11(c), 29 U.S.C. 660(c); Clean Air Act Amendments of 1977, 312(a), 42 U.S.C. 7622(a); Federal Water Pollution Control Act Amendments of 1972, 507(a), 33 U.S.C. 1367.

17. M. H. Malin, "Protecting the Whistleblower from Retaliatory Discharge," *University of Michigan Journal of Law Reform*, 1983, 16(2):277–318.

18. Bureau of National Affairs, *Occupational Safety and Health Reporter*, 13 June 1990, 38.

19. Occupational Safety and Health Administration, "Advance Notice of Proposed Rulemaking: Generic Standard for Exposure Monitoring," 53 *Federal Register* 37591 (1988); id., "Advance Notice of Proposed Rulemaking: Medical Surveillance Programs for Employees," 53 *Federal Register* 37595 (1988).

20. Schulte and Ringen, "Notification of Workers at High Risk," 485–91; Bayer, "Notifying Workers at Risk," 1352–56; Bureau of National Affairs, "High Risk Notification: Questions, Controversies Remain as House Action On Milestone Legislation Nears," *Occupational Safety and Health Reporter*, 7 October 1987, 813–16.

21. Employee Health and Safety Whistleblower Act, H.R. 3368, 101st Congress.

22. M. Witt and S. Early, "The Worker as Safety Inspector," *Working Papers* 1980, 21–29; R. Kasperson, "Worker Participation in Protection: The Swedish Alternative," *Environment* 1983, 25(4):13–43.

23. New Jersey Hazard Elimination through Local Participation Act, Assembly no. 2832, 1990.

Chapter 9

1. J. Page and M. W. O'Brian, *Bitter Wages* (New York, 1973).

2. American Conference of Governmental Industrial Hygienists, *Threshold Limit Values and Biological Exposure Indices for 1988–1989* (Cincinnati, 1989).

3. B. I. Castleman and G. E. Ziem, "Corporate Influence on Threshold Limit Values," *American Journal of Industrial Medicine,* 1988, 13:531–59.

4. Ibid.

5. S. A. Roach and S. M. Rappaport, "But They Are Not Thresholds: A Critical Analysis of the Documentation of Threshold Limit Values," *American Journal of Industrial Medicine,* 1990, 17:727–53.

6. G. E. Ziem and B. I. Castleman, "Threshold Limit Values: Historical Perspectives and Current Practice," *Journal of Occupational Medicine,* 1989, 31(11):910–18.

7. B. Mintz, *OSHA: History, Law, and Policy* (Washington, 1984), chapter 2.

8. For a prominent example, see Brodeur, *Outrageous Misconduct.*

9. 29 U.S.C. 655(b) (5).

10. Industrial Union Dep't v. Hodgson, 499 F.2d 467 (D. C. Cir. 1974).

11. Mintz, *OSHA: History, Law, and Policy.*

12. Exec. Order No. 11,821, 3 C.F.R. 1971–75 Comp., p. 926; Exec. Order No. 12,044, 3 C.F.R. 1978 Comp., p. 152; Exec. Order No. 12,291, 3 C.F.R. 1981 Comp., p. 127.

13. Industrial Union Dep't v. American Petroleum Institute, 448 U.S. 607 (1980).

14. Occupational Health and Safety Administration, "Final Rule: Identification, Classification, and Regulation of Potential Occupational Carcinogens; Conforming Deletions." 46 *Federal Register* 4889 (1981).

15. E. D. Olson, "The Quiet Shift of Power: Office of Management and Budget Supervision of Environmental Protection Agency Rulemaking under Executive Order 12,291," *Virginia Journal of Natural Resources Law*, 1984, 4:1–80; Morrison, "OMB Interference with Agency Rulemaking," 1059–74.

16. International Agency for Research on Cancer, *IARC Monographs on the Evaluation of Carcinogenic Risks to Humans*, World Health Organization, supplement 7 (Lyons, France, 1987); U.S. Department of Health and Human Services, National Toxicology Program, *Fourth Annual Report on Carcinogens*, Publication NTP 85-001 (Research Triangle Park, N.C., 1985).

17. Oleinick, Fodor, and Susselman, "Risk Management for Hazardous Chemicals, 179–278.

18. Occupational Safety and Health Administration, "Final Rule: Air Contaminants." 54 *Federal Register* 2332 (1989).

19. American Federation of Labor–Congress of Industrial Organizations, *Post-Hearing Brief on OSHA Proposed Standard on Air Contaminants*, 31 October 1988.

20. J. C. Robinson, D. G. Paxman, and S. M. Rappaport, "Implications of OSHA's Reliance upon TLVs in Developing the Air Contaminants Standard," *American Journal of Industrial Medicine*, 1991, in press.

21. D. G. Paxman and J. C. Robinson, "The Regulation of Occupational Carcinogens under OSHA's Air Contaminants Standard," *Regulatory Toxicology and Pharmacology*, 1990, in press.

22. Ibid.

23. U.S. Department of Labor, Bureau of Labor-Management Relations and Cooperative Programs, *The Role of Labor-*

Management Committees in Safeguarding Worker Safety and Health, BLMR 121 (1989).

24. J. Mendeloff, *The Dilemma of Toxic Substances Regulation: How Overregulation Causes Underregulation* (Cambridge, Mass., 1988); S. A. Shapiro and T. O. McGarity, "Reorienting OSHA: Regulatory Alternatives and Legislative Reform," *Yale Journal on Regulation*, 1989, 6:1–63.

25. 53 *Federal Register* 32591 and 32595 (1988).

Chapter 10

1. For an exposition of the exit strategy and its link to contractarian social theory, see Epstein, "In Defense of the Contract at Will," 947–82.

2. *Economic Report of the President* (Washington, 1987), 179–208.

3. The tendency for exit strategies on the part of some consumers to lower, rather than raise, product quality has been noted elsewhere, as in the deterioration of public school quality subsequent to the transfer of the most concerned parents to private schools. Albert Hirschman develops a similar analysis and points out: "Competition in this situation is a considerable convenience to the manufacturers because it keeps consumers from complaining; it diverts their energy to hunting for the inexistent improved products that might possibly have been turned out by the competition.... The competitive mechanism then rids management of its potentially most troublesome customers" (*Exit, Voice, and Loyalty* [Cambridge, Mass., 1971], 26).

4. This notion of a "musical chairs equilibrium" can be ascribed to R. B. Freeman, "Individual Mobility and Union Voice in the Labor Market," *American Economic Review Proceedings*, 1976, 66(2):361–68.

5. No one describes the irony of libertarian labor market philosophy better than Karl Marx, who observes:

This sphere that we are deserting, within whose boundaries the sale and purchase of labour-power goes on, is in fact a very Eden of the innate rights of man. There alone rule Freedom, Equality, Property and Bentham. Freedom, because both buyer and seller of a commodity, say of labour-power, are constrained only by their own free will. They contract as free agents, and the agreement they come to, is but the form in which they give legal expression to their common will. Equality, because each enters into relation with the other, as with a simple owner of commodities, and they exchange equivalent for equivalent. Property, because each disposes only of what is his own. And Bentham, because each looks only to himself. The only force that brings them together and puts them in relation with each other, is the selfishness, the gain and the private interests of each. Each looks to himself only, and no one troubles himself about the rest, and just because they do so, do they all, in accordance with the pre-established harmony of things, or under the auspices of an all-shrewd providence, work together to their mutual advantage, for the common weal and in the interest of all.

On leaving this sphere of simple circulation or of exchange of commodities, which furnishes the "Free-trader Vulgaris" with his views and ideas, and with the standard by which he judges a society based on capital and wages, we think we can perceive a change in the physiognomy of our dramatis personae. He, who before was money-owner, now strides in front as capitalist; the possessor of labour-power follows as his labourer. The one with an air of importance, smirking, intent on business; the other, timid and holding back, like one who is bringing his own hide to market and has nothing to expect but—a hiding. (*Capital*, vol. 1 [1867; New York, 1967], 467)

6. The spillover of innovative union programs to nonunion firms is discussed by Kochan, Katz, and McKersie, *Transformation of American Industrial Relations*.

7. S. H. Slichter, J. J. Healy, and E. R. Livernash, *The Impact of Collective Bargaining on Management* (Washington, 1960).

8. R. B. Freeman, "The Exit-Voice Tradeoff in the Labor Market: Unionism, Job Tenure, Quits, and Separations,"

Quarterly Journal of Economics, 1980, 94:643–73; Freeman and Medoff, *What Do Unions Do?*

9. G. A. Akerlof, A. K. Rose, and J. L. Yellen, "Job Switching and Job Satisfaction in the U.S. Labor Market," *Brookings Papers on Economic Activity, 1988,* 1988(2):495–582.

10. G. M. Duncan and F. P. Stafford, "Do Union Members Receive Compensating Wage Differentials?" *American Economic Review,* 1980, 70:355–71.

11. Freeman and Medoff, *What Do Unions Do?*

12. C. Summers, "Democracy in a One-Party State: Perspectives from Landrum-Griffin," *Maryland Law Review,* 1984, 43(1):93–118.

13. Freeman and Medoff, *What Do Unions Do?* 210.

14. The role of nonmarket institutions in supporting market economies has been a central concern of contractarian political philosophy throughout the modern era. The solutions proposed by Hobbes (absolute monarchy) and Locke (religious sanction) are unattractive today. The legal strategy owes much to the solution proposed by Hume, who emphasized the role of precedent and the common law in restraining force and fraud. See D. Gautier, "David Hume, Contractarian," *The Philosophical Review,* 1979, 58(1):3–38.

15. R. L. Abel, "A Critique of Torts," *UCLA Law Review,* 1990, 37:785–831.

16. Klare, "Public/Private Distinction in Labor Law," 1358–1422.

17. Freeman and Medoff, *What Do Unions Do?* 232.

18. P. Weiler, "Promises to Keep: Securing Workers' Rights to Self-Organization under the NLRA," *Harvard Law Review,* 1983, 96(8):1769–1827.

19. Ibid.

20. J. Rawls, *A Theory of Justice* (Cambridge, Mass., 1970).

21. This analysis has been developed in detail by Mendeloff, *Dilemma of Toxic Substances Regulation.*

22. Viscusi, *Risk by Choice.*

23. Heckscher, *New Unionism.*

24. Bacow, *Bargaining for Job Safety and Health.*

25. Page and O'Brian, *Bitter Wages.*

Index

Compositor: BookMasters, Inc.
Text: 10/13 Aster
Display: Helvetica Condensed
Printer: Maple-Vail Book Mfg. Group
Binder: Maple-Vail Book Mfg. Group